Healing Your Church Hurt

What to do when you still love God
but have been wounded by his people

STEPHEN MANSFIELD

BARNA

AN IMPRINT OF TYNDALE HOUSE PUBLISHERS, INC.

Visit Tyndale online at www.tyndale.com.

TYNDALE is a registered trademark of Tyndale House Publishers, Inc.

Barna and the Barna logo are trademarks of George Barna.

BarnaBooks is an imprint of Tyndale House Publishers, Inc.

Healing Your Church Hurt: What to Do When You Still Love God but Have Been Wounded by His People

Previously published as *ReChurch: Healing Your Way Back to the People of God* under ISBN 978-1-4143-3328-1.

Healing Your Church Hurt first published in 2012.

Designed by Beth Sparkman

Published in association with the literary agency of Esther Fedorkevich, Fedd and Company, Inc., PO Box 341973, Austin, TX 78734.

The Library of Congress has cataloged the original edition as follows:

Mansfield, Stephen, date.
  ReChurch : healing your way back to the people of God / Stephen Mansfield.
     p. cm.
  Includes bibliographical references.
  ISBN 978-1-4143-3328-1 (hc)
  1. Church membership. 2. Ex-church members. I. Title.
  BV820.M22   2010
  248.8'6—dc22   2009052959

ISBN 978-1-4143-6560-2

Printed in the United States of America

18   17   16   15   14   13   12
 7   6   5   4   3   2   1

Contents

Foreword

THE UNITED STATES IS A HUGE, POPULOUS NATION. As such, it is
home to numerous epidemics. One of them is the dreaded, but wide-
spread *ecclesia exitus* disease—the Latin term for church dropout.
Perhaps you've experienced it—the decision to permanently with-
draw from a congregation you had considered to be your "church
home." The symptoms are many, but the outcome is unambiguous:
pain, disappointment, and spiritual anomie.

Personally, I've had several bouts of *ecclesia exitus* over the years.
In one case, it was caused when our pastor disagreed theologically
with something that I wrote in a book. Rather than confronting me
personally—the practice he taught from the pulpit, based on Matthew 18—he chose to avoid me and instead go public with his disenchantment. And he didn't do it by just bad-mouthing me to a few
of the faithful: he wrote an entire book on the subject, using me as
his unknowing, voiceless foil. When I asked him why he had not
contacted me first to discuss his concerns so that we could resolve

our differences as mandated in Matthew 18, his response was that if I had a problem with his approach, well, tough luck. Shocked and wounded by the hypocrisy of his actions, and his unwillingness to engage in further conversation regarding his actions, my family and I sought another church to call home.

In another instance, I was serving in a leadership capacity at a church when the senior pastor became uncontrollably jealous of the national attention that my ministry was receiving. He froze me out of leadership meetings and regular processes, and made comments about me to other congregational leaders that were both untrue and unfair. Because he was not willing to admit to me that these things were happening, and other people in the congregation were becoming increasingly upset by the odd behavior of their pastor, it seemed that the most honorable thing for me to do was leave that body. Although the environment had become toxic, it was still a crushing blow for me and my family.

Another instance stemmed from how a predominantly white, affluent congregation treated my Hispanic daughters. All of my daughters are adopted, and two of them are from a Latin American country. While my wife and I were welcomed with open arms by the congregation, the distasteful treatment accorded to our little girls in their Sunday school classes—by teachers and students alike—made it impossible for us to stay put. Once again, the gap between what was preached and what was practiced made it unbearable for us to remain in our church home.

All of these examples are recalled simply to say that I understand the pain involved in being chewed up by a church—a place where you go to worship God, to become more Christlike, to serve others, to enjoy positive relationships with other Christ followers, and to have a safe and reliable place to bring truth seekers for exposure to biblical principles in thought, word, and deed. It can be a shattering reality when your "church home" becomes a place of rejection and suffering while you are doing your best to be part of the spiritual family. It turns your world upside down, births a variety of spiritual doubts, and leaves a sour taste in your mouth.

If you think about it, though, the causes of *ecclesia exitus* have been afflicting the Lord's people since the beginning of church history.

+ Jesus was sent to save the Jews, whose leaders rejected and conspired to orchestrate His murder, in defiance of the spiritual laws and principles that they taught fellow Jews.
+ Paul's letters were written to churches that were distorting the principles provided by Jesus and consequently hurting many people through the misapplication of His truths and admonitions.
+ The description of five of the seven churches depicted in Revelation 2 and 3 reflect congregations that did a poor job of handling Jesus' teachings—and God's people.
+ Even the early church leaders were guilty of infighting and bitterness. Paul had a less-than-amicable parting of ways with John Mark and Barnabas despite a successful initial missionary journey.

Conflict and interpersonal pain are as old as humanity. Perhaps not surprisingly, such difficulties have been present in the Christian Church from its origins, and are likely to be part of every human institution until the end of the age.

Our contemporary culture certainly fans the flames of *ecclesia exitus.* Think about the way in which millions of people interpret fundamental Christian principles and behaviors. Grace is interpreted by many as a weakness to be exploited. Compromise is seen as a loss of substance or courage. Discernment is criticized as intolerance. Blame and retribution are preferred to forgiveness and mercy. In our society, behaving with kindness and humility is often considered with disdain: the choice of losers and wimps.

The paradox inherent in all of this is that the inconsistencies and harshness of our society often drive us toward the most tangible and widely promoted expression of Christianity—the local church, an assumed oasis of perfection and goodness, a place where sinners are transformed into reasonable facsimiles of Christ Himself. But that expectation is often shattered. After all, the local body of believers is still a collection of sinners seeking a place where they can discover wisdom, truth, grace, healing, and love. No local church will ever be perfect as long as people are part of it. In our thirst to experience the righteousness of God, we sometimes forget that we have the capacity to wound others, even in a spiritual environment, as well as a higher-than-desirable probability of being wounded by a community of faith.

Spiritual injury occurs in churches more often than we would like to admit. My research among unchurched adults reveals that nearly four out of every ten unchurched people (37 percent) in the United States avoid church life because of bad past experiences in a church or in relation to churched people. Whether the issue is the judgment rendered against them by churched people, the lack of trust between congregants and church leaders, perceived hypocrisy in the lives of the churched, or outright incivility or meanness suffered at the hands of other church members, some 25 to 30 million adults stay away from Christian churches because of the past treatment they have experienced from the local body of Christ.

Too many adults have contracted *ecclesia exitus* because of how they were treated by the church community during difficult times—after a divorce or sexual affair, in response to rebellious children, because of substance abuse, due to living an unbiblical lifestyle, and the like. The people who were called on by God to represent Him as lovers and healers failed. Those who bore the brunt of that failure took their pain elsewhere, seeking acceptance, understanding, and wisdom from places that simply cannot provide such a balm. But it's all they had available. The church of Jesus did not behave like Jesus the Savior.

Sometimes people leave the local church because they did not get the God experience they were so desperately seeking. Again, my national studies have shown that close to one out of every four adults regularly feels disappointed by the worship services at the churches they attend; about three out of ten adults feel as if they rarely or never connect with God or sense His presence at worship services; and more than one-third of self-identified Christian adults rarely or never feels as if the worship service at their church turns out to be the most important experience they have had all week.

The sting of disenchantment is felt more heavily by some than others. Young adults are especially likely to feel let down or hurt by a church. The same goes for Hispanics and men. And people who are refugees from Catholic and mainline Protestant churches are more likely than those who have participated in other Christian faith communities to suffer from their past experience with churches.

In the midst of the emotional and spiritual upset that occurs when a church hurts or disappoints us, we tend to lose sight of the fact that the local church is merely a collection of people on a challenging journey—a group of people who are involved in a long-term transformation process. We fail to see many churched people as more godly today than they were in the past; still imperfect, yes, but making slow progress toward becoming more godly. Consequently, these works-in-progress become the target of ugly labels and derisive comments. "Hypocritical." "Judgmental." "Narrow-minded." "Holier than thou." And worse . . .

As those pronouncements become more comfortable, sometimes we adopt unreasonable expectations of the body of Christ. When those unfortunate expectations are combined with our culture's general disinterest in facilitating change that takes substantial time and effort, we get disastrous results. One such result is the growing proportion of young adults who drop out of church during their twenties. Currently, 61 percent of people who were churched during their adolescent and teen years drop out of Christian churches when they reach their twenties. Some of them return when they have children, when they get over themselves, or when their hurt has healed enough to give organized religion another chance. But millions of young adults never get that far. Once they leave, they are gone for good. And the proportion of those who are "gone for good" is growing.

Put it all together and it paints a rather dismal portrait of the American church. But that's why Stephen Mansfield's words are so important—both for those who have left the church and for those who have never left. Stephen, another kindred spirit who has suffered through his own bout with *ecclesia exitus*, graces us with the benefit of his years of reflection on the experience. He reminds us that because we are the Church—the aggregate body of believers bound together by our common love of Christ and each other—we are influenced in more ways than we may realize by the presence of this disease.

If you want a resource that merely sympathizes with you over your unfortunate encounter with a church, this may not be the book you are seeking. Stephen's well-considered advice is that you need to deal with the things you can control, and that puts the focus squarely on you. Stephen is not out to beat you up or to engage in "blaming the victim," but his words provide a dose of tough love for all of us: both those who have been hurt and those who have inflicted the hurt. He will encourage you to not simply run from the experience, rewrite it, or contract amnesia regarding the relevant difficulties. Instead, he'll help you dive deep within your heart, mind, and soul to ascertain the best way for you to handle your own pain and doubt.

Personal growth is often preceded by hardship. Jesus even promised that heartbreak and persecution would be part of the journey to wholeness. Stephen Mansfield's words will put all of that in better perspective as you try to make sense out of the role of the local church in your life. It is vital that each of us remains immersed in the community of faith to benefit from the growth potential that can only emerge from being in a relationship with other Christ followers. I believe that this book will enable you to do so with greater enthusiasm, wisdom, and contribution.

George Barna
VENTURA, CALIFORNIA
JUNE 2009

Prologue

YOU ARE LIKELY READING THIS BOOK because you believe that you have been hurt by a church or you know someone who has. Or perhaps you were forced to witness a hurtful church fight, and the experience has wrenched your soul ever since. Whatever the case, there was an incident, a turning point, and since then you have been different.

Things were probably good at the beginning. You joined a church and felt at one with it all. You belonged. You had, perhaps for the first time in your life, that band of brothers we all need, that loving sisterhood that makes life feel complete. So you invested. You sang in the choir or you worked on staff or you assisted the pastor or you raked leaves in the yard. You cared. You prayed. You made this body your own.

Then *it* happened and you've been running the facts over and over again in your mind. There was the turning. Perhaps you should have seen it coming. There was a change in spirit, a look on someone's face, or an unsettling feel to a crowd. And the stormy season came. Maybe it was merciful and quick and private. Or it may have been that long, public, and humiliating kind. But it happened. The storm spit you out like a slowing tornado in Kansas and you have never been the same.

Since that time you've tried to move on but you cannot let it go. You replay the facts in your mind but that only deepens the wound. You wish you could reclaim who you were before the blows came but you do not want to go back to that hurtful time and place. So you simmer in the toxins of your bitterness. And it hurts. God knows, it hurts.

You reach for relief. You find a gang of similarly damaged friends and you drink and you cuss. Or you lose yourself in busyness. Or you eat yourself to peace, but at night you still feel the burning acid reflux of the toxins in your soul.

It may sound like I'm taunting you. It may sound like I'm accusing you of fault or smirking at your pain. No. Regrettably, I 've seen it before. The fact is you are walking a well-worn path.

Here is all I ask of you for now: agree with me that you are not as you should be. I'm not asking that you change your version of the facts or jump back into church or even become the good little praying/Bible reading/smiling Christian you once thought you should be. All I ask is that you agree that the state you are in is not the right state of your life, that something is wrong and has been since the season of the storms. Your body tells you and the face you see in the mirror tells you and the turbulent sea inside you tells you that this posture, this condition, this current molding of your life is not as it should be.

It is as though there is a splinter working its way to the surface, only this splinter is in your soul. And just as the skin wants a foreign object gone and pushes it out, the soul wants to be healthy and will not leave you in peace until you stop drenching it with the poisons of your feelings about the past.

All you need to do for now is agree that you are not whole and have not been since that day. This is the beginning. For we have not met here to whine about what they did to you or teach them all a thing or two. We are here to turn our hearts toward healing, knowing that we cannot continue as we are.

Be brave, then. Tell yourself the truth. Declare the reality of what has happened to you. And then you'll be ready for what comes next.

CHAPTER 1

The Image of Our Folly

ONE OF THE DEFINING IMAGES OF MY LIFE first announced itself when I was twenty-two. At the time I was the director of a dormitory at a major university in the Midwest. My job was to tend the dorm life of several hundred men and to scurry about the campus in response to the many urgent messages that buzzed the pager I carried on my belt. Because this was back in the Dark Ages, the pager was the size of a small house, made a noise like a jet engine each time it went off, and seemed to dominate my life in nearly every way.

One of these urgent messages came on an April morning and sent me rushing to the university's sports complex. The message was followed by a code indicating the matter was serious—paramedics were on the way.

When I arrived, the scene was near madness. My attention was first captured by a dark-haired, attractive woman. I say she was attractive but I have to admit that this was a guess on my part, for the truth is that she was hard to see. She kept bending at the waist, covering her face with her hands, and wailing, "Oh, my God! Oh, my God!" at an ever-increasing volume, as though she had just discovered the presence of evil in the world. I had no sooner taken her in, when a short, balding man charged at me, his finger violently jabbing into my chest, while he yelled that I would suffer the tortures of the damned in court. "I will sue you, your mother, and this university for all you're worth!" the man raged. To this day I'm not sure why he threatened my dear mother, but that is exactly what he did.

Just beyond the wailing woman and the jabbing man was a university security guard. I'm fairly sure that at that moment he was quietly celebrating the university policy that prevented him from dealing with the public. He stared at me blankly, yet with one eyebrow slightly raised as though to say, "It's all yours, bubba. Let's see what you can do."

At the center of this bedlam was Timmy. I knew it was his name because his beanie baseball cap, his matching sweatshirt, and yes, even the socks that rose from his saddle shoes to just below his neatly pressed shorts all sported the word: *Timmy*. And Timmy was in trouble.

I knew that Timmy was in trouble because he was screaming as loudly as any child ever has. The source of his trouble seemed to be that his right arm had been swallowed by a candy machine. There was Timmy with his shoulder jammed up against a huge machine; from time to time, he would angrily try to pull his arm free but couldn't. Then, too, there were those trickles of blood that were working their way down Timmy's arm, threatening to stain the sleeve of the sweatshirt that bore his name.

It was the blood that seemed to incite the aggrieved cries of the woman, who, I soon understood, was Timmy's mother. She would point at the blood, return her hands to her face, wail with the grief of the ages, and commence bending at the waist. The man, of course, was Timmy's father, and in the time-honored manner of men, he expressed his concern for his son by finding another man and threatening him. The man he chose was me.

As a well-trained college dorm director, I had absolutely no idea what to do. Still, taking stock of the four people in front of me, I decided my best chance was with Timmy. I walked over to him, ran my hand up his arm into the candy machine to determine what was really happening, and tried to be comforting.

It was then that I noticed it. Timmy's arm was taut in a way that suggested perhaps he wasn't really stuck after all. By then the paramedics had arrived, but I waved them off.

I stepped back from the screaming boy, looked him firmly in the eye and said, "Son, let go of the candy bar." The mother stopped her wailing. The father backed away from my right ear, in which he had been screaming for several deafening minutes. The paramedics and the security guard looked at me as though I had just denied Christ on the cross. Everyone went silent, waiting to see what would happen next.

And Timmy, mercifully quiet for the first time, pulled his hand out of that machine.

I stepped back from the screaming boy and said, "Son, let go of the candy bar."

I can picture an adult Timmy years later telling a crowd at a cocktail party how that machine walked across the room, sucked in his arm, and wouldn't let go. But it didn't happen that way. All of that commotion and fear, all of that screaming and rage, was because Timmy had a death grip on a Snickers bar.

I cannot tell you exactly why, but God has brought that image back to me again and again throughout my life. Maybe because that screaming boy—the one who threw everyone into turmoil because he refused to let go—has often been me. When I have had my seasons of darkness in my otherwise blessed life, God has used Timmy to remind me that nothing can keep my soul in bondage except the forbidden or unclean thing I insist on holding tight.

It is an image that has served me well. When life has bled me dry or friends have failed me or I have fouled my nest through my own folly, I remember that better days always lie ahead if only I will loosen my Timmy Death Grip on what I should have left alone in the first place: my offenses, my bitterness, my need for revenge, my anger, my self-pity, my pride.

Never was this lesson and the image of Timmy more vital to my soul than when I found myself in the middle of a good old-fashioned church fight. For nearly a decade, I had been the pastor of a growing and influential church. It had been a glorious experience and I had loved the life that we shared and the history that we made as this nearly four thousand-member congregation pursued the things of God. But then, for reasons that don't need airing here, it all came to an end amidst conflict and uproar. Oh, it was a classic—complete with a conspiring church board and gossip packaged as "sharing" in prayer meetings and accusations flying fast and loose. Demons danced and angels wept, and I should say quickly that I sinned, too. But for the record, I did not shoot John F. Kennedy, I did not create global warming, and I did not offer Adam and Eve the forbidden fruit.

Frankly, it was a soul-deforming season of hell, and it ended with me leaving the church I had led for more than a decade, suffering all the isolation and suspicion that such departures usually entail. I was stunned by the humiliation, lashed by the loss and the loneliness. Each morning when I awoke, I had to remember what was happening to me, my soul so fractured at the time. And when it was all over, it wasn't over. Though I thought I had gone through all the required horrors and had begun to move on, I soon found that those horrors kept cycling through me.

This is when the real horrors began. The sheer force of what I had experienced and my foolish habit of constantly replaying it all in my mind shoved me off balance and began squeezing me in a vise of pain and hostility. I was becoming a sour, angry, dangerous man. In my agony, I could justify almost any moral choice and in my mind somehow make that choice a jab at my enemies and, yes, at God. He, after all, had allowed all this to happen.

It got worse. I wanted them to die. All of them. The ones who had hurt me, the ones who liked the ones who had hurt me, and the ones who sat silently by while the other ones hurt me. I wanted them to die and die horribly, and I wanted to do it myself.

Nothing can keep my soul in bondage except the forbidden or unclean thing I insist on holding tight.

And when that murderous rage turned inward, I began to plan my own death. In desperation, I had gone to a monastery to pray and try to recover. It was a horrible decision. I had chosen to do this in the dead of winter. Everything was brown and frozen. And the facilities were, well, monastic. It was just after Christmas, no one was around, and since the place was run by Trappist monks bound by a vow of silence, no one would talk to me. It was a depressing experience on top of my already depressing experience. On the drive home, I imagined how peaceful it would be to let my car drift into the path of an oncoming truck.

I was a mess. It had happened not just from the bludgeoning of the initial church fight, but from my ignorant decision afterward to let my soul become a toxic bog. I was spoiled little Timmy and I had a death grip on my own version of the forbidden candy bar—a life-deforming bitterness.

It was at that moment that some men, by the grace of God, stepped forcefully into my life. They were pastors, but pastors of an exceptionally bold and unapologetic kind. I would like to tell you that they sweetly and gently led me to truth. They didn't. They nearly beat me to death. It didn't matter to them that I had pastored a church of thousands. They didn't care. They called me an idiot, told me that I'd better grow up, and then they proceeded to take me apart, one unclean piece at a time. It was torturous, unfair, embarrassing, and rude. And it set me free.

What I learned during that rough season of soul surgery is found on the pages that follow. More important for the moment is what I experienced as I emerged clean and free: adversity, endured righteously, has the power to lift a man to new heights.

Or as George Whitefield said, "A man's suffering times are his best improving times."

Or as Hebrews 12 indicates, hardship is God's discipline in preparation for a better day.

However you say it, the lesson is the same: if you do the hard thing the right way, you become a better person. And by the grace of God, I did.

Shortly after my long, dry season, God opened a new and surprising phase of life for me. He allowed me to begin speaking around the world. He made it possible for me to write books on vital topics and some of those books became international best sellers. He gave me influence in the corridors of power in our nation, and he allowed me to help shape, in very small ways, some of the major events of our time. After more than two decades of pastoring a church, God still allowed me to pastor people, only now I did so from behind the scenes.

I do not recount these opportunities to make myself seem grand. I've already admitted that I'm a knucklehead, and I realize that anything I have achieved has been due to God and others. But it is important that you know who I became so that I can describe to you what I began to see.

It is universally true that the experience of one man exerts a magnetic pull on the similar experience of another man. Pain, I assume, calls to pain. Victory calls to victory. I suppose people who have been abused in some way can sense it in others even if no words are spoken. I imagine the rejected can instantly sense rejection in others, or those who have conquered some fierce moral flaw in themselves can quickly identify those of equal character nearby.

Perhaps because of this truth about the human experience and perhaps because God wanted me to learn what will fill these pages, I began shortly after my dark season to experience what can only be

> *Adversity, endured righteously, has the power to lift a man to new heights.*

called a grand tour of the religiously wounded. It was inescapable and profound.

My first book as I stepped into my new life was *The Faith of George W. Bush*, which was a best seller and made me welcome among some of the politically powerful in our country. Time and again, though I would say nothing about the subject, well-known men and women began talking to me about what they had suffered at the hands of their fellow believers and how it had marred their lives. Sometimes the issues were petty. One national leader told me how he had left his Episcopal church in anger over the placement of a bike path. At other times, the issues were a bit more substantial. A very powerful man I came to know well had left his church because the cross on the church wall was replaced by a video screen. The man, known for his angry approach to politics, had clearly been damaged by the experience. And then there were the tales of cruelty and spite. One of the most powerful CEOs in America wept with me in his office as he recounted how fellow church members distanced themselves from him when he was vilified in the press. Another, a handsome white man, married a beautiful black woman but then found his church home of decades alienating them because of the mixed marriage. This man was a visible national leader, but the experience of religious spite has left him distanced from his past, his God, and even parts of himself ever since.

After my book on President Bush's faith, I wrote another called *The Faith of the American Soldier*, which required that I go to Iraq to find out what was happening in the religious lives of the U.S. troops there. It was a glorious experience for this Army brat, but again, the theme of hurt in church emerged often. There was the brave chaplain who spent an hour telling me how the church he pastored back home had pledged to keep him as their pastor while he was at war only to remove him months later and treat his wife harshly. This chaplain planned to leave the ministry after his tour of duty was done.

There were also stories that circulated among the young soldiers, members of a generation already suspicious of "organized religion," that made them cling to God but hate the church. Again, some of it was petty: disagreements over styles of music, a favorite minister who was fired, or a bitter feud about the building fund. However, some soldiers were the children of clergy who had witnessed bloodlettings over politics in the pulpit, pastors being fired without severances, a leader's family suffering an entire community's ire over a single sermon, and incessant church infighting that ultimately led to heart attacks, divorce, crippled souls, and scuttled churches.

These were weighty matters, and their anger seemed justified. But then, even as I continued to listen compassionately, I also heard these young warriors speak with just as much heat about matters that seemed trivial. One soldier told me how he left a church when the leaders decided to pave the parking lot. An airman told me of his church splitting over the worship team's insistence on wearing jeans, and another spewed rage over his pastor's insistence on using the New International Version of the Bible rather than a version more to his liking.

In time, I became aware that what is important is not so much the *cause* of the offense, but rather the common characteristics of the offended soul itself. No matter the size or importance of the event that had led to the offense, I encountered a poisoned soul. In each case, a soul was distanced from God. In each case, a leaking toxic bitterness was tainting everything that soul touched. In each case, morality, vision, and love suffered.

These common characteristics of the offended soul knew no bounds. I had the privilege of going to the Vatican and ended up talking to a priest over pasta about his harsh treatment by a superior. I lectured at the United States Military Academy and found a high ranking officer who "loved God but hated his people" and planned to "do my own religious thing" for the rest of his life. While sitting in a Starbucks drinking a chai latte and reading a book, I ended up in a conversation with a young man who took certain scandals among famous preachers so hard you would have thought the wrongdoings were personally directed at him. In each case, no matter the cause, the condition of the soul was the same.

> No matter the event that had led to the offense, I encountered a poisoned soul.

And I remembered Timmy. I remembered the candy machine that held him bound. And I remembered that Snickers bar.

I came to the conclusion that no matter how large or petty the cause, every religiously wounded soul I encountered was in danger of a tainted life of smallness and pain, of missed destinies, and the bitter downward spiral. And every soul I encountered had the power to be free, for each of them, no matter how legitimately, was clenching the very offense or rage or self-pity or vision of vengeance that was making life a microcosm of hell.

I understood. I understood it all. I knew what it was to want to serve God and to be so naive and eager that when the blows came you could not breathe for the pain. I knew what it was like to lay awake all night thinking about the good days and the tender talks and the laughter that promised friendship for a lifetime and to wonder where it all had gone. I too had thought so hard about the harm to my children and the carpet bombing of my life that I sometimes made myself ill.

Then there was the problem of God. Every person whose story I heard was wrestling with God or with his will or with the fact that his children could be so cruel. Some tried to dismiss it all by refusing to believe any longer. Others drifted, suspended somewhere between unknowing and doubt, but none would ever approach God the same way again.

I do not mean to overstate, but it did not take me long to see this religious offense syndrome as a plague. I was stunned by what had been lost to the Christian church through offended people slipping away. When my friend George Barna told me that in fifteen years, present trends continuing, church attendance in America will be half of what it is today, I knew immediately that much of this had to be as much due to offense and wounding as it was to the other factors Barna identifies so well. This is happening at a time when the gospel in America is under vicious attack and when the state of the world cries out for a vibrant, whole, passionate church to tend its woes and lead it to truth.

So we come to this book. Both friends and publishers have asked, "Why would an author of books on popes, presidents, and prime ministers write a book about getting over your church hurt?" I told them what I've told you here: that the poisoning of souls through church hurts is killing us. That the cause of Christ is hindered because the body of Christ is bruised. That most of the Christians I know either believe they've been wronged by a church or have friends who do.

That some of these confessions have been among those presidents and prime ministers I write about. And that some of the most gifted and potentially powerful Christians I know are right now at a Starbucks or at a bar somewhere griping about the church, too tainted by grief and bitterness to be of any use to anyone.

> Every person whose story I heard was wrestling with God. None would ever approach him the same way again.

I want to bring them home. I need them. You need them. I'm tired of seeing the best souls of my generation bearing the mark of Cain, rootless wanderers roaming the earth thinking they can never go home again.

When I consider how I might accomplish this, I'm reminded of a story. A guy falls into a deep hole and starts yelling for help. Soon a doctor happens by and hears the anguished cry. The doctor peers down into the hole, writes a prescription, throws it to the guy below, and keeps walking. Before long a priest comes by and he peers into the hole. Seeing the man below, the priest writes out a prayer and throws it down before walking on. The guy in the hole starts yelling even louder. Soon his friend Joe comes by.

"Hey, Joe, help me. I'm down in this hole."

So Joe jumps down into the hole too.

"What have you done?" our guy says. "Now we're both stuck down here!"

"Yeah," says Joe calmly, "but I've been down here before and I know the way out."

And I do. I know the way out, not because I'm smarter or holier than anyone else. I know the way out because I fell harder and deeper than most people do. Perhaps my only saving grace was that I also yelled harder and longer for help than most people do.

I know what you or your wounded Christian friends have been through. I know what it is like to drive the streets on a Sunday morning, unable to attend your usual church but too embarrassed to attend a new one.

I know what it is like to meet old friends on the street and to feel the faint chill, the uncomfortable distance, as they quizzically search your face for some trace of the evil that caused those other folks to treat you so horribly.

I know what it is like to sit up all night rehearsing conversations that you will never have with friends you will never see again about events that only you seem to remember.

I know what it is like to play the scenes over and over again in your mind only to conclude that the whole thing was your fault, too, and then to get so depressed about it all that you wonder why God doesn't destroy his church in some new kind of flood and start all over again.

I know what it is like to think that the warm ooze at the bottom of a bottle or the warm skin you aren't supposed to touch or the mountain of food or the nasty Web site or the angry band of brothers will soothe your soul's need.

I know.

I know, too, because I have a Timmy nature that is spoiled and childish and won't let go of what it wants no matter the turmoil it creates, no matter the pain it inflicts on me and others.

I know the way out, and if you are going to follow me out through these pages, you are going to have to understand three important truths.

First, I'm not your counselor. I'm your coach. If you want to sit around discussing the psychology of spiritual abuse there are plenty of books on the subject, but this isn't one of them.[1] If you want to talk about Mom and Dad and your dysfunctional family and how you hoped for more from the church, there are plenty of folks who have hung out shingles to have just such a conversation with you, but I'm not one of them.

I want to show you how to get clean and free from what you have done to yourself in your church hurt. That's it. Along the way we are going to talk a bit about how to be part of a church without surrendering your soul and what healthy churches look like. But I'm not trying to fix the body of Christ. I'm trying to get you to fix what you can in you, so that God can fix the rest and get you back into the fold.

Counselors nurture souls. Coaches teach skills. I'm your coach.

Second, I want you to understand that you will not get free unless someone gets tough with you. When we are in pain, we have too many voices playing in our heads—voices from the past, voices of our critics, voices of our admirers, and even the voice of our own inner dialogue. There are likely some other voices from demons we have known and loved. More about this later. Suffice it to say, a riot is taking place in our souls when we hurt. All of this tends to make us distracted at best and crazy at worst. We need someone to cut in harshly and silence the storm.

Remember those 1950s movies in which every time a woman got a little flighty somebody would reach up and slap her hard across the face? It was weird, I know, but sometimes that is exactly what we need in the stormy swirl of our pain. In a sense, this book is written to be a slap in the face. It is a one-on-one between you and me and I'll spare you nothing because the only way I got free was to be spared nothing by men who loved me. Don't read any further if you're not willing to endure a little pain.

Finally, there is a myth that we need to knock in the head—and we need to knock it in the head now. When we've been hurt by the church we often tell ourselves that we are going to keep on loving Jesus but that we no longer want anything to do with his people. We say this to ease our pain but we are fools when we do. First, the Bible makes it clear that we cannot love Jesus and hate his people. First John 4:20 boldly states, "If anyone says, 'I love God,' yet hates his brother, he is a liar. For anyone who does not love his brother, whom he has seen, cannot love God, whom he has not seen." To think that we are entitled to love God and hate his people is sin. And, perhaps as important, it is impossible. Frankly, when we think we are loving Jesus but hating his people, we are actually loving Jesus so little that his people don't matter anymore.

> *When we think we are loving Jesus but hating his people, we are actually loving Jesus so little that his people don't matter anymore.*

But there is a second reason this "love God, hate the church" approach is doomed, and you must get this straight. Here's the mystery: Jesus has a thing for his bride. From the

Song of Solomon to the book of Revelation, the truth of Scripture is that Jesus loves his bride the Church. There's just no getting around it and we ought to stop trying.

We really shouldn't be surprised. This is the way it is among us mortals, as well. If you are going to be my friend, you have to at least be pleasant to my wife. I'm wild about her and you can't mistreat her and expect to be close to me. You just can't come to my house to hang out with me and eat my food and soak up my air conditioning but ignore my wife. The same is true of Jesus. He loves his bride. Go figure. She's a mess in my view, but he's crazy about her and won't put up with me either speaking ill of her or pulling away from her if I'm going to be intimate with him.

That's why this book is no "what-bad-things-those-church-people-did-to-me" memoir. Nor is it a guide to "go-it-alone" Christianity. The fact is that if you are going to love Jesus, you're going to have to make nice with his wife. To intend otherwise is pride, and you need to decide now whether you want to live what Jesus calls the Christian life or if you're going to make up some new religion called "Salvation My Way."

> *If you are going to love Jesus, you're going to have to make nice with his wife.*

Decide. Now. And, then, if you're ready, let's get on with it.

One more thing: My focus in these pages is on you and how to get you whole. I cannot judge between you and the church that you believe did you harm. I'm going to talk about your church hurt and, yes, I may allude to how abusive some churches can be. But do not misunderstand: I am not the judge in a lawsuit. I am not the mediator in your dispute with whatever organization wronged you. I am someone who nearly let his offense with the church ruin his life, and I am putting these words on the page to help you avoid the same sad mess.

I'll take it a step further. You have been replaying the facts of your situation over and over again in your mind. You want to talk about the facts as you see them, and then you want to set those facts afire and shove them into the faces of those who wronged you. But hear me on this: there may be a time and a place for the facts to be aired, but getting the facts right will never set you free. Even if everyone involved in your hurtful situation instantly agreed with your perspective on the facts, it would not heal the damage that has been done to your insides. So, excuse me while I sidestep the facts—your version and theirs—and simply show you the path to wholeness. Then, may God do with the facts of your painful situation whatever he pleases.

So now, once again, when you're ready, let's get on with letting go of your candy bar.

CHAPTER 2

The Sea Breeze
of the Centuries

LET ME TELL YOU A MYSTERY OF LIFE in this world. When we
hurt, we walk alone. Or at least we think we do. Our pain tells us
that we are unique among all people and that others cannot understand and do not wish to draw near. We search the faces of those we
pass by and wonder if they have ever known agonies like we endure.
We conclude that they have not, that no one has, and so we decide
that we alone are wounded wanderers in the earth.

It is this loneliness that deepens our suffering. Our isolation tells
us we are somehow damaged and this is why we have been abandoned. This only increases our sense of guilt for the hardships we have
brought on ourselves and others. We feel like the sheep who strayed
from the flock and is now lost and shivering in the cold, untended by
the shepherd and unable to draw near to the fire in the night.

What we wish for is companionship, and not just the near-
ness of bodies but the companionship of common experience. We
want to know that someone understands our journey, shares our

perspective on what we've endured. We want an experience—not unlike discovering the still-warm embers of a campfire when we are lost in the woods—that allows us to say, "Someone has trod this way before."

This is why in our darkest hour, in our most gut-wrenching seasons, it may be the past that brings us the greatest comfort and the greatest encouragement to soldier on. Think about it. In the tumultuous times of our lives, the future is—as always—unknown to us, and in our pain it may appear more fearful than ever. The present, of course, is the scene of our current suffering. The past, though, tells us the tales of those who have gone before. The past offers us examples of men and women who have faced even greater horrors than ours and yet have lived such lives that we remember them today. The past whispers to us that "Noble souls of days gone by can show you the chosen way." This is why C. S. Lewis wrote that we should allow the "clean sea breeze of the centuries" to blow through our lives.[2]

Yet the comfort we might receive from the past is often limited by how little of that past we know. We have likely been taught history as the stories of statues, as the Pageant of the Grand whom we commemorate in stony monuments. This version of history is pristine and ordered and bland. It is dates and dead people. Seldom, though, are we shown the back story, the down and dirty, the agonies that the greats of history endured. So when we contemplate the lives from history's hall of fame, we rarely see them as anything more than disapproving symbols of what we ought to be and are not. We find it hard to locate anything in their experience to which we can relate and from which we can draw wisdom and inspiration for our lives.

Consider this. There once was a very overweight child who also happened to be a stutterer. His father, descending daily into madness, despised this child and refused him any affection. This child grew into a young man who failed miserably in school and brought his parents no end of embarrassment. He was in debt every day of his adult life. His marriage was troubled. One of his children committed suicide, one drank himself to death, and one died in infancy. For a season, he was among the most despised men of his country, largely because he once made a decision that spilled horrific suffering upon his countrymen. And even when he became the leader of his nation, he suffered such "black dog" depressions that he refused to stay in a room with a balcony attached for fear that a depression might strike him and cause him to hurl himself from that balcony to his death.

It occurs to me that we might not hire a man like this for the most menial job, and yet I am speaking of Sir Winston Churchill, arguably the greatest leader of the twentieth century. You see, because we did not know what he endured, we could not draw from his story the power it has to offer us.

Some fear that it diminishes our heroes of history to know their failings and their miseries. The truth is that it endears them to us and makes them our companions. For example, some of us have hard marriages and wonder if we can still achieve anything of note. Consider Abraham Lincoln. On the day when Lincoln was to be married, he abandoned his bride at the altar. When friends went to find him, they discovered him in bed fingering a pocket knife and contemplating suicide. It was not a good start.

Fifteen years later, a carpenter came to the Lincoln home. After being there for just a few minutes, the carpenter had put up with all he could from Mrs. Lincoln, who was famous for being difficult. The carpenter went to Lincoln to complain. The future president put his huge, rail-splitter hands on the man's shoulders and said, "Surely you can endure for fifteen minutes what I have endured for fifteen years!"[3]

But let's not limit our stories to political leaders. The pages of church history are full of similar tales that make us laugh, comfort us, and inspire us to live lives of consequence. John Wesley, the great founder of the Methodist church, helped lead England in such a revival that it probably kept that nation from a disastrous French-style revolution. Yet his marriage was horrible. A friend who went by the Wesley home to accompany John to a meeting found Mrs. Wesley dragging the revered preacher around the house by his ponytail! Indeed, it was not uncommon for Mrs. Wesley to show up at one of her husband's meetings—to heckle him while he preached!

Do we think less of Wesley for his troubled marriage? Are his achievements any less grand, the lives he has touched through the generations any less transformed because he was human, because he did not have the perfect marriage? No. In fact, we breathe a sigh of relief that perfection is not the only door to significance. And we can face our troubles with new strength precisely because while Wesley was great, Wesley was also failing at home.

This, then, is why I begin this book urging you not to look first inward, but to the past; to turn your face into that "clean sea breeze of the centuries" that C. S. Lewis so loved. There you will find that you are not alone, that men and women have endured far worse than you have at the hands of their fellow Christians and have lived lives of worth afterward. There, in the pages of history, you will laugh in relief at the follies of humanity and weep for the pain and the cruelty, but you will not feel alone. And as we continue our journey of restoration you will know that the price is worth paying.

Let us consider, for example, the life of George Whitefield. He was one of that band of gifted men who, along with John Wesley, led England in the great revival of the 1700s. Indeed, he was so influential in early American history that some have called him our "Forgotten Founding Father." Yet most Americans barely know who he is or even how to pronounce his name. It is "Wit-field" and not "Whitefield" as the spelling suggests.

George Whitefield was born in Gloucester, England, and later attended Oxford University where he had a dramatic conversion experience under the tutelage of John and Charles Wesley. Sensing a call to ministry, Whitefield began to preach—and those who heard him knew that God had given him something special. His ability to preach was so piercing and the Spirit of God so strong upon his life that he drew crowds of astonishing size from his earliest days as an Anglican clergyman. One sermon in London's Hyde Park was attended by over eighty thousand people.

Men and women have endured far worse than you have at the hands of their fellow Christians and have lived lives of worth afterward.

Yet as stunning as his success was, equally stunning was the opposition that arose against him. Whitefield began his ministry during one of the great times of spiritual darkness in British history. It was during the Gin Craze, when one in every six houses was a Gin House and signs advertised "Drunk for one penny, dead drunk for two pence, clean straw for nothing."[4] One Anglican bishop complained, "Gin has made the English people what they never were before—cruel and inhuman."[5]

The upper classes of English society were cynical at heart and removed from the needs of the age. Meanwhile, the church made little difference in the lives of those in its charge. The French jurist and philosopher, the Baron de Montesquieu, perhaps said it best when he visited England in 1731 and reported, "A converted minister is as rare as a comet."[6]

So as Whitefield called men to Christ, he endured the most blistering criticisms which, in turn, fueled violence against him. It was not uncommon for him to record in his journal, "I was honored with having a few stones, dirt, rotten eggs and pieces of dead cats thrown at me." At one meeting a man tried to stab him to death. At another, opponents hired a drummer to drown him out. He was beaten, his pulpits were smashed, and on several occasions cattle were driven through his audiences. He even preached one sermon while a man tried to urinate on him.

Some of the most famous men of the age attacked him. William Hogarth, the renowned artist whose prints give us a window into the character of eighteenth-century England, mocked Whitefield in two engravings, one called *St. Money-Trap*.[7] Poet Alexander Pope compared Whitefield's "harmonic twang" to the braying of an ass, and playwright Samuel Foote parodied "Mr. Squintum"—Whitefield had an oft-mentioned lazy eye—as a "blockhead dealing in scriptures as a trade."[8] Even the eminent Samuel Johnson joined the fray. Refusing to "allow much merit to Whitefield's oratory," Johnson insisted that the evangelist's "popularity . . . was chiefly owing to the peculiarity of his manner." Johnson suggested that Whitefield "would be followed by crowds were he to wear a nightcap in the pulpit, or were he to preach from a tree."[9] It is important to remember that all of these critics were Christians.

As virulent as his opponents were, though, none of them kept Whitefield from his passionate pursuit of souls for God. Yet a day of real wounding came, and when it did, it came at the hands of his friends.

John Wesley had long disagreed with Whitefield over the doctrine of predestination. Wesley leaned more to free will while Whitefield built his theology more on the choices of a sovereign God. The two had remained close despite their distance on theology, until, that is, Wesley thought he heard God say that he should "print and preach" against the views of his friend.

While Whitefield was proclaiming the gospel throughout the American colonies—on one of seven tours he would make in his life—Wesley began a campaign against predestination. He printed a sermon entitled *Free Grace* that painted Whitefield's doctrines in such hellish terms that many who were converted under Whitefield in the revival began to wonder if the man who led them to Jesus might be a heretic. The tens of thousands who once lauded Whitefield as their father and a champion of the faith now turned against him.

We can hear the pain of the experience in Whitefield's words. When he returned home from America, he discovered that "many of my spiritual children, who at my last departure from England would have plucked out their own eyes to give them to me, are so prejudiced by the dear Messrs. Wesleys' dressing up the doctrine of Election in such horrible colors, that they will neither hear, see nor give me the least assistance."[10] Instead, many of his converts sent "threatening letters that God will speedily destroy me."[11]

There were tearful nights. There were hours of crying out to God in anguish. There was the weakened health and the tormented mind that the gall of bitterness leaves. Yet, finally, Whitefield rose above his pain to be the man he had long prayed to be.

Had he not, it might have been the end of both the revival and his passion for God. He might have begun to nurse a defiling bitterness and this might have cost him the strong anointing on his life. He might have fought back against his former friend and torn the great movement of renewal in two.

He did none of these things. Instead he forgave his friend, spoke lovingly of him to others, and made sure his own astonishing success in ministry reflected glowingly on Wesley. In time, he even gave Wesley the buildings he had constructed to house his thriving ministry. He also refused to allow any movement to grow up in his name but instead urged his followers to become Methodists under Wesley's leadership. His constant refrain was, "Let the name of George Whitefield perish so long as Christ is exalted."[12]

We can read such episodes from the past and fail to take stock of the hurt and the damage almost done. Whitefield was only human and yet he was publicly and harshly betrayed by his father in the faith. The result might have changed the course of nations and tainted God's work for years to come. Instead, Whitefield rose above. And God gave him a larger field. By the end of his life, not only had he led transforming revivals in Scotland, Wales, England, and the American colonies, he had also influenced some of the greatest men of his time. His impact on the founding generation in America alone was beyond any other. John Adams once wrote, "I know of no philosopher, or theologian, or moralist, ancient or modern, more profound, more infallible than Whitefield."[13] And Benjamin Franklin, who had long been impressed with Whitefield and worked to make him a friend, wrote to his brother what surely echoed in the hearts of many of his day: "He is a good man," Franklin admitted, "and I love him." Thus George Whitefield surmounted the wounds he sustained from fellow Christians in order to live for a higher cause and the hope of deeper impact on his times.

Yet Whitefield was not alone in the betrayal by the church. The pages of Christian history are full of such episodes that great men and women of God had to endure before becoming what we know them for today.

Consider the story of St. Patrick. This bold, unflinching man of God transformed the nation of Ireland with the gospel of Christ. Had he been a lesser man and succumbed to the pain of betrayal by a friend, it might never have happened.

Patrick was born in Britain late in the fourth century. Though his father was a Christian deacon and his grandfather was a priest, Patrick admitted that he had not yet believed in Christ for himself when at the age of sixteen, Irish raiders kidnapped him from his home. For six years he worked as a captive herdsman, miserable and ill-fed in the often chilly pastures of Ireland. Yet during this bondage, he found his way to Christ. He spent his days in song and prayer and knew an intimacy with Jesus that transformed his life. When he finally did escape, he returned to Britain determined to become a priest.

After he was ordained in 417, Patrick astonished his friends by deciding to return to Ireland—the very land where he had been a slave. He explained that he had heard the voice of God calling him to set the captives free in that largely pagan land. His fearlessness, his supernatural gifts, and his earthy ways of expressing spiritual truth won the Irish chieftains over to his God and led to the conversion of thousands. Patrick changed the lives of the Irish people and through them, the course of the world.

Just when Patrick was winning his most glorious victories for Christ, a nasty, undermining church fight almost distracted him from his cause. Reading about it all these years later, it is hard to believe how such a small matter nearly overthrew the progress of this heroic man.

It seems that during the years Patrick was studying for the priesthood in Britain, he had made a confession of sin to a friend. This was the standard practice among clergymen in training and it was understood that anything confessed in private was meant to stay that way. Yet thirty years later, the friend to whom Patrick had confessed decided to make the matter known to the church. And those who were jealous of Patrick or who were grasping for control of his work used this confession against him.

It is clear that Patrick was wounded by this betrayal and disgusted at the valuable time he had to devote to defending himself—time better spent winning a nation. Patrick's famous *Confession* is filled with the details of this controversy nearly as much as it is with the record of his thrilling conquest of Ireland. We can hear the surprise and hurt in his own words.

They brought up against me after thirty years an occurrence I had confessed before becoming a deacon. On account of the anxiety in my sorrowful mind, I laid before my close friend what I had perpetrated on a day—nay, rather in one hour—in my boyhood because I was not yet proof against sin. God knows— I do not—whether I was fifteen years old at the time, and I did not then believe in the living God, nor had I believed, since my infancy; but I remained in death and unbelief until I was severely rebuked, and in truth I was humbled every day by hunger and nakedness. . . .

Hence, therefore, I say boldly that my conscience is clear now and hereafter. God is my witness that I have not lied in these words to you.

But rather, I am grieved for my very close friend, that because of him we deserved to hear such a prophecy. The one to whom I entrusted my soul! And I found out from a goodly number of brethren, before the case was made in my defence (in which I did not take part, nor was I in Britain, nor was it pleaded by me), that in my absence he would fight in my behalf. Besides, he told me himself: "See, the rank of bishop goes to you"—of which I was not worthy. But how did it come to him, shortly afterwards, to disgrace me publicly, in the presence of all, good and bad, because previously, gladly and of his own free will, he pardoned me, as did the Lord, who is greater than all?

It is almost beyond belief. A man is kidnapped by barbarians and while in captivity turns to Jesus Christ. He miraculously escapes and returns to his homeland to prepare for a life of ministry. As a student, he confesses to a friend a sin that he committed before he had even believed, a sin from a decade before. Then, thirty years later, this friend brings this sin before all the church, and Patrick, who is successfully evangelizing Ireland at the time, is embarrassed and hurt. There are meetings to review Patrick's qualifications for ministry. His moral life comes under scrutiny. And this mighty man of God is reduced to defending himself in his fifties for a sin he committed when he was fifteen.

We can imagine how deflating this must have been. We can picture the disillusionment, almost feel Patrick's agony. To be risking your life daily in taking a nation for God and then have the bureaucrats back home debating and nitpicking every detail of your life. To be questioned about your morality when you have shown nothing but good character for decades. How humiliated Patrick must have been, maybe even to the point of wanting to simply walk away.

Yet, like Whitefield, Patrick rose above the enemies of his soul. As we read his story, we find that he forgives, says he is concerned for the betraying friend's soul, and then ultimately appeals to being forgiven by Jesus Christ. Though the church leaders would go on to spend years astir in this matter, Patrick lovingly leaves them to their pitiful debates. He returns to the business of changing lives in Ireland and becomes, in time, the greatest name in that land.

Here is the lesson: Great men and women of God are not exempt from hurt and offense. Instead, enduring the wounds of fellow Christians with mercy and grace seems to be the call of every true saint, and we should not expect it to be any different in our own lives.

Indeed, it seems that the greater a man is in God, the more opposition from fellow believers he is forced to endure. Consider the story of Jonathan Edwards. Perhaps the greatest theologian America has ever produced, Edwards was also one of the leading pastors in the colonial era. And he was a genius. He entered Yale at the age of thirteen, graduated at seventeen, and by the tender age of twenty-four had replaced his revered grandfather, Solomon Stoddard, as the pastor of the famed Northampton Church—one of the leading churches in the American colonies.

Young as he was, Edwards proved he was up to the job. Preaching such fiery sermons as the famous "Sinners in the Hands of an Angry God," he led the Northampton Church in a renewal of spiritual passion that was recounted throughout the English-speaking world. Stories circulated widely of how sinners moaned and cried out their repentance before God while Edwards preached. A spirit of repentance fell upon the people, and before long Edwards was reporting that the town was filled with the glory of God, that a visitor walking down the street could hear songs of praise sounding forth from every house. It was marvelous, and when the famous George Whitefield came to preach at Northampton Church, Edwards and his congregation realized that the revival in their town was part of a larger work of God throughout the colonies, one that historians would come to call The Great Awakening.

Enduring the wounds of fellow Christians with mercy and grace seems to be the call of every true saint. We should not expect it to be any different in our own lives.

Yet more than souls were awakened during this great work. Evil was as well, and as a result, Edwards—theological genius, beloved pastor, and leading revivalist—would eventually find himself in the fight of his life.

The conflict arose because of Edwards's commitment to biblical truth. He had read Paul's words in 1 Corinthians 11 that a man ought not to partake of the Lord's Supper unworthily; instead, he should examine himself and see if he was truly right with God. For Edwards, this meant that he should not allow the unconverted to take Communion and, when he announced this decision to his congregation, he found himself fiercely opposed. There were, in Edwards's words, "crafty designing men" who were "professors of religion yet not the most famed for piety," who "used their utmost endeavors to engage the minds of the common people in this controversy."[14]

There were meetings and arguments. Committees pondered by the hour and the whole town seemed stirred in debate. And when it was all thoroughly considered, the revered Jonathan Edwards was voted out of his church.

It was an astonishing blow. The greatest theologian and pastor of his age was fired from the church he had served well for decades. And it grew worse. The church's board had failed to find a replacement in advance, so in his humiliated, discredited state, Edwards was forced to preach for another six months before the very people who had voted sent him away. His daughter was so upset by it all that she refused to sit with the congregation the few times she went to church.

The folly of it all was confirmed by the account of some visitors who attended Northampton at this time. These men had heard stories about Edwards and had determined he must be an evil influence. They were glad he had been voted out. They attended the church to check out Edwards's replacement, and thought he did a magnificent job. In fact, during the sermon, one of these men turned to the other and said, "This is a good man." Then, in a few moments, "This is a very good man." And finally, after a while, "Whoever he may be, he is a holy man." But of course it was Edwards himself whom these men heard. Though wounded and rejected by his people, he was still, indeed, a very good man.

And the pain of it all, a kind of pain that has echoed in the lives of many a man and woman of God, is evident from Edwards's words to a friend: "I have now nothing visible to depend upon for my future usefulness or the subsistence of my numerous family. But I hope we have an all-sufficient faithful, covenant God, to depend upon."[15]

In time, a new position came, this time in Stockbridge, out on the Massachusetts frontier. Again, Edwards was committed to being a faithful pastor and set himself to the work of God. And again, there was conflict. A controlling family named Williams disliked what they'd heard about Edwards through the years and decided to oppose the famed minister's every move. They complained about the way he ran a school for the Mohawk Indians and about the way he preached and about the fact that he didn't honor the wealthier families as he should. But Edwards knew the truth: "There has for many years appeared a prejudice in the family of the Williams against me and my family, ever since the Great Awakening in Northampton 18 years ago."[16]

Finally, in appeal to the governor, Edwards pitifully wrote, "The ruin of my usefulness and the ruin of my family, which has greatly suffered in years past, for righteousness sake, are not indeed things of equal consideration with the public good. Yet, certainly, I should first have an equal, impartial and candid hearing before I am executed for the public good."[17] These are the words of a strife-weary, oft-opposed man, yet they are also the words of a man who has not lost his passion in a righteous fight.

In the end, Edwards prevailed. Indeed, he not only served well in Stockbridge, but later went on to become a president of what is now Princeton University and one of America's greatest men. He did not lose his faith. He did not succumb to the smallness and the hate that his church fights might have left in his soul. And on the day of his death, when doctors thought he slept for the last time, he leapt to consciousness and asked, "Now, where is Jesus of Nazareth, my true and never-failing friend?" Then, a few moments later, he calmly said to all in the room, "Trust in God, and you need not fear." They were the last words he ever spoke in this world and the enduring message of his life, a truth proven in conflict after conflict in this noble man's service to his God.

Whitefield. Patrick. Edwards. Each a man of great impact in the history of the church. And each a man whose potential for higher usefulness might have been lost to bitterness and strife. This is what history teaches us: that opposition from Christian friends is often the price of the calling of God.

Yet someone might object that all three of these were preachers and that it is easier for them. They have to make nice, after all: have to answer kindly when their fellow believers slam into their hearts. Though this isn't necessarily true, let's look now at some people who weren't preachers and still managed to keep their faith after deep disappointment with the church.

Consider the life of Vincent Van Gogh. We know him as the painter of such magnificent works as *The Starry Night*, *Irises*, and the Sunflower series, as well as his haunting self-portraits. Yet few know of his vibrant Christian faith and of the nearly life-deforming disappointments handed down to him by his church.

He was born in 1843 to a Dutch family that had given the world pastors and theologians for generations. Around the age of thirty, Vincent had a deep evangelical conversion and was known to read the Bible and sing hymns by the hour. He devoured Christian books like John Bunyan's *Pilgrim's Progress* and Thomas à Kempis's *The Imitation of Christ*, and he found inspiration in the work of famed English preacher Charles Spurgeon and the American revivalist Dwight Moody.

Vincent soon felt a calling to become a pastor, and he asked tutors to help him prepare for the university work he would need. It did not come easily. His fiery mind would not settle down to the Greek and Latin studies that seminary required. In 1878, he was refused admittance to the Theological Faculty of Amsterdam.

It was an agonizing disappointment, but after a time of confusion and grief, he simply chose another way. He decided to live among the coal miners in a town named Borinage and to model for them the way of his Christ. He was determined "to preach the Gospel to the poor and to all those who needed it." In the little mining town, he preached and gave Bible lessons but refused any of the privileges usually accorded to pastors at the time. Instead, he decided to live in opposition to all luxury. In short, he renounced all. He slept on the floor and lived without soap—at times not even bathing. He ate little and often looked less healthy and more ragged than those he wanted to help. When typhoid fever broke out in the district, Vincent gave everything he had to the sick miners. He was trying to live out what he had learned—from the example of Jesus, from à Kempis, from the mystics of history he so admired.

When an inspector from the official Dutch church made a visit, he chastised Vincent for his excessive zeal. He found the young missionary emaciated and worn out and lying on a sack filled with dirty straw. Starving, suffering miners crowded around Vincent fearing he might die. The church inspector could stand it no longer; he not only ended Vincent's financial support but also ordered him to go home.

Vincent became angry, embittered. He thought he had done what Jesus called him to do and was stunned that the church would disagree. The experience skewed his view of Christianity and for a while he nearly lost his faith. Living in his father's home for a time, he refused to attend church. His passion for God drained away, and in his disappointment with Christians, he even began reworking the tenets of Christianity in his mind.

But there came a day of return and, though Vincent Van Gogh never lost his suspicion of religious hierarchies and the institutional church, he did come home to his faith and to a God who had called him to reveal the beauties of God's creation. Van Gogh went on to paint dozens of biblical scenes throughout his life with a tenderness that revealed his spiritual devotion to the world. And even in later years, when depression and madness ruined his life, he would find his greatest comfort in painting Jesus and the biblical scenes that had come to mean so much to him.

It is a pattern we have often seen. Van Gogh sought to serve God. Van Gogh was hurt by the church. Van Gogh recovered himself and lived to reveal his God in greater ways. And so it was with all the men we have seen. Their stories confirm that the Christian life means sustaining hurt—a hurt that sometimes comes from those who share your faith.

So it is today. Indeed, though we can think of thousands of examples of church-wounded, church-weary people in our contemporary world, let us just look at one: that wild, unruly, thrilling, gifted man named Bono, the lead singer of U2.

Bono was born Paul David Hewson in the Ireland of the 1960s. The death of his mother when he was still a teenager plunged him into a spiritual crisis, and he took comfort in a loose evangelical gathering called Shalom that met for song, worship, and Bible study. He left the group, though, when the meetings became too structured.

This might have been the end of Bono's connection to God. His artistic, nonconformist soul did not thrive in system and ritual, was not fed by a regimented spiritual life. He might well have moved away from God while moving away from what the church offered him. But somehow this young man found a middle way. He grew to love God and honor his church but sustain his faith in a variety of expressions.

"I just go where the life is, you know? Where I feel the Holy Spirit," Bono has explained. "If it's in the back of a Roman Catholic cathedral, in the quietness and the incense, which suggest the mystery of God, of God's presence, or in the bright lights of the revival tent, I just go where I find life. I don't see denomination. I generally think religion gets in the way of God."[18]

Rather than become embittered, Bono drank from the varied streams of his Christian faith. And later in life, when he used his fame to become a global conscience on the matter of AIDS, this largeness of heart kept him once again from offense with the church. In trying to awaken slumbering Christians worldwide to the plague in their midst, he might have grown angry at their selfishness, wounded by their lack of response. But refusing such smallness, he pleaded with an open heart: "This generation will be remembered for three things: the Internet, the war on terror, and how we let an entire continent go up in flames while we stood around with watering cans. . . . Let me share with you a conviction. God is on his knees to the church on this one. God Almighty is on his knees to us, begging us to turn around the supertanker of indifference on the subject of AIDS."[19]

And though he felt his cause so keenly and though he struggled daily with the church's slow response, he continued to keep his heart open—to God and to the frailties of humanity—and he did not pull away and he did not fail to love. And this is why he is one of the greatest spokesmen for faith and social conscience today. This is why we see him in those famous photographs: Bono standing with the Pope, Bono standing with Rick Warren, Bono standing with Billy Graham, Bono with the Archbishop of Canterbury, Bono with every kind of leader of faith. He has not let himself become offended with the slowness and larded structures of the church. Instead, he connects to the church broadly and loves his God while he strives to do the good that his astonishing fame allows.

Surely it is odd to put a man like Bono beside great leaders of old like Whitefield or Patrick or Edwards, or even an artist like Van Gogh. But the issue here isn't their style of leadership or even the age in which they lived. The issue is the condition of the human heart, which does not change from age to age and which is tender to the wounding blows no matter the man or when he lives. This is what these men have in common: they have all conquered being wounded and disappointed in order to make their mark for God.

The vital message here is that you are not alone. When you think of that great cloud of witnesses that Hebrews 12 describes, you must not think of them as perfect saints who never suffered as we do. Instead, you must see them as the flawed and the betrayed and the wounded who simply chose to live above the programming of their pain. Just as you can.

It may be hard for you to believe this. Having been chewed up and spit out by the church, perhaps you believe that the destiny you felt for your life is lost, that you will never achieve the greatness your heart reaches to. But this is a lie—unless you choose to live small. Unless you choose to give in to the bitterness and the rage. And this is the lesson you most hold dear: The confirmation of history is that we are not called *despite* our wounding and betrayal; we are wounded and betrayed *because* we are called. And God yearns to make your pain redemptive in your life.

> God yearns to make your pain redemptive in your life.

So, again, you are not alone, but you do have a choice and it is time to make that choice now. Will you sink into the swamp of cynicism and hate, or will you follow the example of the saints of old and let your hurtful experience become a tool in the hand of God? This is the critical question, one that I ask you to ponder urgently as you read the pages to come.

CHAPTER 3

Man: The Greatness and the Grief

SHE IS THE CHURCH, THE BODY OF CHRIST, the bride of the Son of God. In the Greek language of the New Testament, her name is *ekklesia*, the "called out ones"—a people drawn from darkness to God and to one another. She is the fulfillment of God's plan for creation and the revelation of God's wisdom to the powers of the age. She is the lover for whom Jesus eagerly awaits, the dispenser of justice and truth the devil dearly fears, and the body of the Christlike called from the nations of the earth.

This is the Church—universal and invisible and pure. She is splendid and glowing, the mystical vision of believers through time.

Now don't you wish you had attended a church like this!

Well, you did. Sort of. You attended the more local version—the visible church, the church small "c." This version of the church meets on a corner and has bathrooms and pews. This church has parking lots, pays its electric bills, and has meetings to decide what to do. Though this church is the people of God first of all, it is also budgets and bulletins, picnics and ushers, and committees for every purpose under the sun.

Yet as mundane as all this may sound—particularly when compared with the glories of the invisible bride of Christ—this visible church is much more than just a building and sign. She is a living being, a gathering of the faithful where God enthrones himself and pours out his grace. She is, according to the picture we have in the book of Revelation, the place where God places his lampstand, his seal of anointing and power. This is the symbol of the Holy Spirit, who flows through our leaders and through the band of believers that makes up each local expression of the body of Christ.

And this is what we feel—that energy or dynamic or flow that permeates everything when we join with fellow believers to worship our God, to live as a community of faith.

It is glorious, isn't it?

To be part of a church, when it is right and good, is to plug into a loving power grid of possibilities and meaning and joy. It is to feel as one at the feet of the Creator and to launch together on missions of eternal weight. Words like *destiny* and *calling* and *gift* fall from our lips as we try to describe how transforming it all is, how we feel like our reasons for existence have found their earthly base.

Sermons seem to sound forth from the throne room of God. We worship and feel ourselves at times lifted as though into heavenly realms. Kneeling at the altar or passing Communion to a friend in the pew, we glimpse what it is for a people to feed on Christ as one. We recite the Apostles' Creed or say the Lord's Prayer or quote a verse with our fellow believers and know what it is to stand together for eternal truth. Classrooms become fountains of revelation and even our mundane labors for the church become sweet offerings on the altar of God.

And through it all the miraculous flows. The sermon on Sunday morning seems to come in answer to our most secret prayers and also prepares us for the questions raised by friends at dinner the following week. The people at church call at just the right moment with just the right offer of help or word of comfort as though dispensed from heaven above. Sometimes it seems almost silly. We flip channels at an odd time of day and land in the middle of a broadcast by some television minister whose words are spoken as though in answer to prayers we prayed only moments before. Then there is the roadside sign or the movie scene that seems to echo in our souls as though sent from another world. Belonging to a church seems somehow to position us to recognize God's words wherever they appear.

It can seem at times like a taste of heaven. We sit in church on Sunday morning and sing the ancient songs, aware that we are voicing the cry of generations and that perhaps saints who now form a cloud of witnesses above are singing along. Or maybe we dance our worship and we sense that Jesus dances at our side. We listen to our pastors or our priests speak the words of God. We have dined with them, even argued and laughed with them. We know they are human. Yet when they stand before the people of God assembled and speak the truth, they are transported. They are more than themselves and we know that it is nothing they have done on their own, but it is God who fills them for our sake.

Our church prays and lost daughters return to their families and warriors come home safe from distant wars. Souls are healed, addictions are broken, and lives are restored by grace. Children are raised in knowledge of the truth, the boundaries of God impressed into the soft clay of their lives. Men are taught to be noble and women are taught to be true and all are taught a fierce faith that pleases God and serves the good of humankind. This is what it means to belong to a church.

Yet church isn't all lofty and sweet. There is also the fun, the rowdiness, the holy play that is the humanity in us touching ground. A child belches in church and says aloud so all can hear, "That was a good one, Daddy!" Everyone remembers the time the pastor dressed like Braveheart or the youth leader roared his motorcycle down the hall. A hymnal falls from the balcony and bops an elder on the head, prompting tearful laughter for weeks after. There is the mud fight at the retreat and the pie-eating contest that got out of control and the time the whole congregation erupted in laughter when the elder said from the pulpit, "Let's all hold up Sister Jensen's leg in prayer."

Then, too, there are the hugs on Sunday mornings and the old ones holding hands and the meals that come when you're sick and can't make it on your own.

And when it works, when it all comes together and there is peace, finding the joy of a good church feels like finding the meaning of life. We wonder that anyone would refuse such a gift and we long for the world to know. "Come," we say. "Know our God and his people, the Church. You are hungry for it whether you know it or not and nothing in a bar or a gang or an entourage can mean what this will if only you come along."

But we are not fools. We know that evil lurks. There is the divorce plaguing the family that usually sits in the fourth row and we see the man who has come to church drunk more than once. We know that the worship leader had to be let go for something troubling not long ago, and we recall sadly the eighteen-year-old who killed himself a few years back. We know that darkness presses at the edge of the light.

Yet here is where we begin to set ourselves up for pain and disillusionment, for in our love for our church and our holy regard for those who lead us in the things of God, we forget the nature of humanity. We are not surprised by the evil pressing in from without, but we are blind to the potential for wickedness that slumbers in our own souls. We forget that humans are a combination of greatness and grief, of righteous might and disgusting sin. In our sentimentality about our church and those we love in it, we forget to stand guard against the natural failings of humanity. We turn off our deflector shields and cast aside our filters and begin to ignore the signals our inner radar may be sending.

When it works, when it all comes together and there is peace, finding the joy of a good church feels like finding the meaning of life.

For you see, in the truth we preach and so adore, there is a description of ourselves we can never afford to forget. Paul tells us in his letter to the Galatians that human beings in their lesser selves are given to factions and discord and jealousy and selfish ambition and dissensions and hate, to name but a few of our darker traits. In other words, sin has hardwired treacherous tendencies into our souls. And they define us, at least until they are rewired by the Word of God, by the Holy

Spirit, and by our own efforts to make ourselves new in Christ. Still, we are never perfect in this life, and even though Paul follows this list with another list he calls the fruit of the Spirit, we surely can see that our lesser deeds—what Paul calls the acts of the sinful nature—are always at war with that higher being we can be by the Spirit's power.

This is so important there is no sense going further until we understand it. Look up from these words and see the people in the room with you. Your spouse in the bed next to you or that man across the room at Starbucks or the couple walking in the park where you are reading—all are good examples. They are probably astonishing beings. They probably have within them beauty and talents that would make the angels weep. God alone knows the potential they have to achieve greatness or change the lives of others. Yet as surely as this is true, it is also a fact that these very people also have the capacity for the vilest deeds imaginable. The level of depravity and nastiness potential in each one would leave you aghast, and yet this is what it means to be human.

Surely we have learned this lesson by now. We know enough history and have read enough in the news to realize that every human is both Beauty and Beast, both Dr. Jekyll and Mr. Hyde, both image of God and image of evil. There is the generous humanitarian who murders his wife and the genius scientist addicted to drugs. There is the preacher who builds a glorious church while at the same time is addicted to cocaine and sex with men. There is the groundbreaking pediatrician who turns out to be a pedophile and the award-winning public school teacher who sleeps with her students. The catalog of darkness never ends.

This is, I'm sorry to tell you, the nature of humanity, and we know this not just by observation but because the Scriptures make it clear from every page. In fact, one of the most endearing features of the Bible is how God chose to portray people without apology in their raw and fallen state. Think about it. David, the very man God calls a friend, is a liar, a murderer, an adulterer, and a thief. Paul, the lion of the New Covenant, reverses his own message on circumcision and speaks bitterly of feeling second fiddle to the other apostles. Peter not only betrays the Lord he has loved and followed for years but also can't decide whether to live as a Gentile or a Jew. Timothy is an astonishing weakling who develops stomach trouble because of his nervous stress. And the Christians at Corinth behave so badly that Paul says they are worse than those who don't believe.

Were these people in our churches today, our critics would call them hypocrites, for they sometimes lived at odds with the truth they proclaimed. Yet this is as all humans are. The difference for us Christians is that we ought to have the firmest grasp on reality, keep the potential of sin always before our eyes, and live in light of the possibilities of evil in our midst—yet without a cynical soul or a frozen heart.

One of the most endearing features of the Bible is how God chose to portray people without apology in their raw and fallen state.

This is what we often forget when church becomes for us an anointed haven, when the grace is flowing and all is well. We become sentimental. In our minds we remake people into what we need them to be. We are not wise in our love, prudent in our commitments, knowing in our fellowship. And so the evil comes and we are first amazed and then destroyed and then knocked off our axis as though never to return.

I have listened by the hour to the tales of what people have suffered as they have endured the blows of human nature in the one place they never expected harm—their church. I am more sorry than I can express. I grieve for them. Yet I also must say that to be surprised that human nature would rear its ugly head—in the very place where it is under the greatest pressure to change, where the stakes are high and the devil strikes hard—is simply biblical ignorance and a failure to live in any sort of connection to the real world.

And so the bludgeoning comes and the tales retold at the coffee shop or the bar carry word of devastation to a world eager for bad news about the church.

"I was a pastor who rescued a failing church and then, after we were going strong, the elders got so jealous that they trumped up a reason to fire me."

OR

"I went to a church where I was the only Democrat and the pastor hated me so much he sometimes mentioned me during his sermon. So, I just left."

OR

"My pastor was downloading sermons off the Internet and preaching them like they were his own and when I called him on it, the deacons got mad at me and ran me off."

OR

"I was on the staff of a church where the pastor kept making inappropriate comments to the young girls and when I mentioned it to him he fired me."

OR

"I was part of the team that helped build our church from a home group to a megachurch, but once we got successful our lead teacher decided he was an apostle and the rest of us weren't and so he asked us to resign. I was disgusted so I left."

OR

"I was a pastor who served my church well but a few ladies began prophesying that I was not of God. One of these ladies was an elder's wife and soon I was replaced for no good reason at all."

OR

"I took my family to what I thought was a good church but my kids weren't welcomed into the cool kids' clique that was led by the pastor's daughter. My son was so wounded he isn't walking with God to this day."

OR

"I gave generously to my church and then I found out that the buildings and property were owned by a single family and that all my giving just made them rich."

OR

"My family helped to start this church when Lincoln was still president, but my increasingly liberal denomination has installed a gay priest and now I can't even go to the church where one of the windows bears my family name."

OR

"My pastor got caught in his office doing inappropriate things with his secretary and when the board found out they just covered it up."

OR

"I committed a sin and confessed it to one of my pastors privately but then one Sunday I found myself rebuked in front of everybody. I'll never go back to church again!"

And so it goes. The stories of wounding and offense could fill a thousand books and still be unfinished.

Yet what we need to know to take our first steps toward healing is this: even a list of wrongs as disturbing as this one is nothing new. It has always been thus, and not just in the more recent centuries of the Christian church. No, from the very moment of its birth, the church has experienced crises and fights of a kind that tempt us to wonder if some of the early Christians knew Jesus at all.

Some would say that this conflict is evidence that Christianity isn't true, that the very fact that early Christians were such messes confirms that the gospel made no difference in their lives. But I believe the opposite is true. If Christianity teaches anything, it is that men are deeply flawed and need rescue. In fact, Christianity even teaches that once we become Christians, we are still merely works in progress. The Bible confirms this when it insists that we were saved, we are being saved, and we will one day ultimately be saved. In other words, even the salvation Jesus brings to our lives is a progression. So it is no surprise to the biblically informed that Christians past and present are screwed up. This, in fact, is confirmation of the gospel.

We should love God for hiding none of this from us in the pages of Scripture. He shows us how flawed we are, even after the gospel has entered our lives, and presents this to us not to disillusion us but to show us the potential of our own damage. The idea is that if we learn well, we can live more effectively.

Let me tell you one of the stories from the pages of Scripture that is astonishing in its raw portrayal of the human capacity for smallness and strife. We first encounter Mark at a rather odd moment. It comes in a short passage at the end of the fourteenth chapter of the Gospel of Mark, following a description of Jesus' arrest in the garden of Gethsemane. The passage is simply, "A young man, wearing nothing but a linen garment, was following Jesus. When they seized him, he fled naked, leaving his garment behind."

It is an odd description, surely one of the strangest passages in Scripture. You will probably never bother to memorize this verse or post it on your refrigerator. Yet it is also one of the most touching verses in the

Once we become Christians, we are still merely works in progress.

Bible when we consider that what we are reading is the remembrance of an older man looking back on one of the defining moments of his youth. The young man, of course, is Mark himself and the words were written years later by a mature Mark who is looking back on his role in the arrest of Jesus. It is a dear memory to him, one that he has often recounted, but it is also perhaps somewhat bittersweet because this was but the first time that he ran away. There would be another time, and it would become one of the most disturbing episodes not only in his life but in the life of thousands of other first-century Christians, as well.

You see, Mark was a very young man during the first thrilling years of the early church. He was likely still in his teens, yet he was privileged to be a witness to some of the great events of the apostolic age. Indeed, some of those events happened in his living room! His mother, Mary, who was probably a widow by this time, owned a house in Jerusalem that often served as a base for the early church leaders. We read in Acts 12:12, for example, that when Peter was miraculously delivered from prison, he made his way to the house of Mary, mother of Mark, where believers had gathered to pray. Scholars also believe that the Last Supper may have taken place in Mary's house and that this is why Mark was wrapped only in a sheet at the arrest of Jesus: soldiers had come to the house to take Jesus away and Mark, who was likely sleeping, had run to warn Jesus wrapped only in his bedding.

Mark, then, had the privilege not only of witnessing the birth of the Christian church but of having Jesus Christ as a guest in his house. This was heady stuff for a mere teenager. Yet we should also remember that Mark was the only son of a widow wealthy enough to own a home in the center of a growing city and to host large crowds in her house. There was no father in the home as far as we can tell, and everything that comes afterward indicates that Mark may well have been a bit spoiled, a bit overmothered, and certainly lacking in the traits that make for an exceptional man.

There is another player in the story of Mark: Barnabas. Paul tells us in Colossians 4:10 that Barnabas was Mark's cousin, though it is obvious that Barnabas was much older than his younger relative.

Barnabas was from the island of Cyprus and was also a Levite, yet what most distinguished him was his character. Luke, the author of the book of Acts, goes out of his way to tell us in Acts 11:24 that Barnabas was "a good man, full of the Holy Spirit and faith." We can also glimpse the love and respect the early church leaders had for Barnabas by the nickname they gave him. His real name was Joseph, but the apostles took to calling him Barnabas, which means "Son of Encouragement," or, more specifically, "Son of Prophecy." This beloved man was likely a prophet who brought so much encouragement and wisdom to the early church that the apostles just didn't think the name Joseph captured all that he meant to them.

The pace of our story quickens with the events of Acts 13. The scene is Antioch where prophets and teachers have come together to fast and worship. While they are ministering to the Lord, the Holy Spirit speaks and says to the leaders, "Set apart for me Barnabas and Saul for the work to which I have called them." It is a historic moment. Saul had once been the persecutor of the Christians and after he was converted, Barnabas had worked hard to win acceptance for Saul amongst a skeptical church. Finally, Paul's faith and works convinced the believers of his genuineness, and he was even made one of the leaders at Antioch. And now he and Barnabas are to go forth as a missionary team to carry the gospel to Asia, a region that was approximately the nation of Turkey today.

It was a thrilling step for the church at Antioch, and once again Mark was honored to play a role. Luke tells us that Mark accompanied Saul and Barnabas as their helper. What an astonishing privilege! Mark, still a very young man, was to accompany two seasoned men of God who were set apart by the Holy Spirit to carry the light of the gospel into the darkness of the Roman world. We can only guess how this came about. Perhaps Mark's doting mother pestered her relative Barnabas into taking the boy along. We can almost hear her pleading: "Please, Nephew! Take the boy! He has lived these years without a father and time with you will be so good for him. Besides, he can be a help to you and Saul. I've taught him well." Or maybe it was a practical choice. Perhaps Mark was strong and could carry the bags or maybe he knew a language the two older men might need. We cannot know for sure. But we do know that Mark boarded the ship with Barnabas and Saul and sailed into the pages of missionary history.

But not for long. As we read this story in Acts 13, we go only eight verses further before we read these words: "Paul and his companions sailed to Perga in Pamphylia, where John [Mark] left them to return to Jerusalem." What! Left them? But it could not have been more than a few weeks! Left them? But why?

Perhaps Mark was spoiled by his wealthy mother and found carrying the baggage and sleeping on the floor too much. Perhaps he got tired of his cousin telling him what to do, though this isn't likely given the reputation Barnabas had for being a kind soul. Then, too, it may have been that Mark was just homesick, that he was a momma's boy who missed his bed and his PlayStation and his mother's huge flat-screen TV.

We don't know for sure, but we do know that Paul was furious. We find out just how furious at the end of Acts 15. After the famed Council of Jerusalem was concluded and all the matters of how Gentiles should become Christians were solved, Paul turned to Barnabas and said, "Let us go back and visit the brothers in all the towns where we preached the word of the Lord and see how they are doing." Barnabas thought this was a great idea, but then he made his mistake. He suggested that they should take Mark with them.

Now, you have to understand that Barnabas was an encourager-type. He was pastoral and loving and as a prophet saw potential in Mark others couldn't see. "C'mon, Paul," he might have said. "The boy has changed. Give him a chance. I think there is greatness in him if we only work with him a bit."

Paul was different from Barnabas. He was an apostle and he could be demanding and impatient. He wasn't the kind of man to suffer fools gladly—and certainly not twice! Mark had burned them just eight verses into their missionary journey, leaving them without help. Paul had to preach, do miracles, *and* carry the luggage—and he hadn't forgotten it. Not for a minute. No, Mark was definitely not going on this second missionary journey if Paul could help it.

The two men, so the Bible tells us, had a "sharp disagreement." This is Holy Spirit code language for a knockdown, drag-out fight. They argued. Voices were raised. Tempers exploded. Harsh words were used. And when it was all over, the two men parted company.

Imagine it with me. Two of the giants of the early church are called together by the Holy Spirit himself to preach the gospel and they end up parting company over what? A snot-nosed, teenaged, momma's boy who was too selfish and spoiled to stick it out more than a few weeks. And all the church knew: it was Mark. He had abandoned them. He had run away—again! He may have even hindered the Holy Spirit's plan with his laziness and his childish ways.

It got worse. Luke tells us that Barnabas took Mark back to Cyprus. Paul, though, left with Silas and was "commended by the brothers to the grace of the Lord." Luke may be hinting at something here. This smells like a split. It sounds like the leaders sided with Paul and blessed him as he continued on his missionary journeys with a new companion. Barnabas, this noble, gentle soul who had been so esteemed by the church, just left. No blessing. No honor. And why should he get the blessing of the church? After all, didn't Barnabas try to force that weakling Mark onto that courageous man Paul? Wasn't Barnabas just siding with a family member, blind to all the trouble that kid had caused?

We must be careful not to miss the heart-wrenching statement at the end of Acts 15, where all this is described. And it would be easy to miss it, because it is what *isn't* there that makes it so heart wrenching. You see, Barnabas is never mentioned again in the book of Acts. In fact, once he set sail for Cyprus with Mark in tow, we never see him again in the New Testament, except in Paul's recollections. This great man—who had given generously of his wealth to the cause of Christ, who had engineered Paul's acceptance by the very Christians he had once persecuted, who had faced the hardships of the first missionary journey, and who had battled valiantly for salvation by faith for Gentiles—this great man sailed to his homeland dishonored, distrusted, and probably despised by some in the church.

There is more to this agonizing tale, but it is best told in later pages. What we must do now is take stock of the extent of this disaster in the first few fledgling decades of the church. Remember that the Council of Jerusalem and this crisis between Paul and Barnabas took place around AD 45, just a dozen years or so after Jesus was raised from the dead and the Day of Pentecost launched the Christian movement. The church was still a babe in the world, during an age of mounting persecution.

In this delicate situation, the crisis between Paul and Barnabas threatened to damage the church for decades. We know that tensions over this matter spilled out into the larger body of Christ. Husbands and wives likely argued at breakfast tables and factions developed, with some believers siding with Paul and others feeling that Barnabas had been wronged. Even churches far beyond the walls of Jerusalem were tainted—we know this because years later Paul had to warn believers as far away as Asia about their attitudes toward the matter, as we shall see.

And, strangely, God spares us none of this. But why? How easy it would have been for him to inspire Luke to write the story of the early church as a glowing tale of triumph and never trouble us with such disturbing accounts of wounding and strife. We might have preferred it—the book of Acts free of any failure or hardship or pain, one victory after another gracing each page.

Yet it would have been a lie. Christianity is not the absence of stupidity and hurt. Christianity is the message of a God who uses our stupidity and hurt to make us what we are destined to be. It is the truth of a God who became like us in order to lift us from our smallness and our spite and make us into a people he is willing to call friends. In short, God is more honest about human nature than we are. He wants us to see it all—the anger in Paul, the stubbornness in Barnabas, the whiny weakness of Mark, and the willingness of the early church to nearly come to blows over the matter—and he wants us to see it on the very pages of Scripture so that we are never astonished by how foolish human beings—and, yes, Christian human beings—can be. It is as though Luke's book should actually be titled The Acts of the Apostles Both Glorious and Vain.

This, then, is the lesson: Christians can be dangerous. We are members of a fallen race, who are being reconstructed through the grace of Jesus Christ. Still, until our day of perfection comes, we are a mixture. We might think of ourselves in terms of that old cartoon image of an angel on one shoulder and a demon on the other. This is actually a concept that comes from Islam and not from Christianity, but it serves our purposes, for there really is a constant tug-of-war going on for our souls. Every Christian has a capacity for the most magnificent Christlikeness. Yet, every Christian also has the potential to commit the most disgusting and horrible acts of the flesh. This is the reality of the Christian life and we fool ourselves if we think otherwise. Perhaps more importantly, we fail to understand what the very basis of our faith, the Bible, so clearly has to teach.

Christianity is the message of a God who uses our stupidity and hurt to make us what we are destined to be.

What this means practically is that the very people we hug on Sunday morning or welcome into our homes for cell groups are beings who both bear the image of God and evidence the scars of evil, who both strive to live the truths of God and yet sometimes descend into the character of pagans. This is the reality—of human nature, of the Christian life, and of biblical truth.

It is a severe mercy to know this. We might be tempted to despair and wonder how Christians can ever live peacefully and effectively together given their flaws, given the darkness that lurks in our souls. How can a church ever be a haven from evil or a pastor ever a safe guide if the potential for harm is as I've described? Yet, I have said that this truth is a severe mercy because it is a mercy indeed and of the most liberating and transforming kind.

It is a mercy because it is reality and any truth that helps us understand the world as it is should certainly be welcomed as a gift. How much we have suffered because we have not known the world for what it is. How much we have endured because we assumed, because we made life over in an image of our choosing rather than lived it as it genuinely is. It is our naïveté, the sentimental gloss we put over the world that leads us to folly and hurt. To know gritty truth about life straight from the pages of Scripture is part of the grace of God and allows us to live safely and effectively in a fallen world.

It is also a mercy because it takes some of the personal sting out of what we have endured. The pain that we have suffered at the hands of Christians may have come through individuals—that pastor or teacher or friend—but it was part of the broader matrix of sin in the world and mixture in the church that is not aimed at us specifically. Though people may have tried to harm you, even their wish to do this evil is part of a darker force that is beyond you and your present circumstances. Yes, people harmed you, but they did so because they were playing out a dark drama that has been going on for centuries. You were wounded at the edge of a broader war that is not about you, and knowing this helps you feel the blows less intensely, take the message of the pain less personally, and defy the "I'm damaged because I'm uniquely cursed" lie with the power of the truth.

Yet, perhaps the greatest blessing of the severe mercy of knowing the lesser side of our nature is that once we know people as they are, we can love them as Jesus does. This sounds contradictory, doesn't it? We would think that knowing people with the evil filtered out, as though they were disarmingly cute Disney characters, would allow us to love them better. But it isn't so, for when we think of them in this way, we are shocked when they misbehave and we stop loving them. We become bitter and disillusioned because we had hoped for better from our fellow Christians. Far better to know people for the cruel creatures that they are, and to love them despite their flaws, than to love them as we wish them to be and constantly be disappointed and hurt.

There is an intriguing verse in the Bible that describes the way Jesus viewed us. At first reading, it sounds surprisingly cynical and cold, but when we put its insights next to what we know about Jesus, we gain a marvelous insight into the true nature of love. John 2:24-25 describes the moment after Jesus had done amazing miracles at the Passover Feast when many people were putting their faith in him. "But Jesus would not entrust himself to them," John writes, "for he knew all men. He did not need man's testimony about man, for he knew what was in a man."

If we didn't know any better, it would be easy to conclude that Jesus was a cold fish—aloof, suspicious, and self-protective. We can imagine him looking at his disciples with a wary eye, wondering inwardly what deceitful thing they would do next. He would doubt any kind words spoken to him and radiate a detached unfriendliness that would repel those around him.

But this isn't the Jesus we know. Let's look at the verse again. The word *entrust* comes from the root of the word that means "faith." In other words, the verse might read, "Jesus did not put his faith in man." In other words, he did not depend on men, need their assessment of him, rise or fall based on their view of who he was. He "knew all men," "knew what was in a man." So he did not base his life on what men said about him. He was a man with a clear sense of self and a clear sense of destiny, and these were unaffected by anything men had to say about him.

Yet to get the full picture, we have to remember that Jesus loved people perfectly—these deeply flawed creatures, upon whose words he did not rely and in whom he did not put faith because he knew what was in them? These are the very people he died for, the very ones he loved so unreservedly that he endured the shame and the cross for their sakes.

This, then, is the key. This is how we do it, how we live in a church of fallen, desperate creatures and love them completely. We love as Jesus did. He knew what was in our hearts, knew the evils and fantasies and wickedness that circle like sharks in the waters of our souls. So he did not base his life, sense of self, or sense of purpose on people's words or admiration. Still, he perfectly loved those he interacted with and even enjoyed them, because he had no illusions about what they could be.

If Jesus sat in your church on a Sunday morning, he would know that the woman in the second row of the choir was a deep believer but was also given to bitterness and gossip. Yet he would worship with her, love her completely, and work in her to make her whole. He would have no illusions about her, nor would he entrust himself to her or let his sense of who he is rise and fall with her opinion of him.

Jesus would also listen to the pastor preach that fabulous sermon, all the while knowing of the porn problem or the anger problem or the troubles at home. Still, he would love and enjoy and let his pleasure rest upon the man. And yes he would strive to heal him though he would not put his emotional or spiritual weight down on the man and his opinions. The same might be true of the bishop or the deacon or the usher or the nice family in the twenty-second row or . . . you.

And we should do no less. For whatever else you believe about the church circumstances that have hurt you and have driven you to this book, you must admit that much of your hurt is your astonished horror that people you trusted could be so cruel. True? And you must own your foolishness in over-trusting, over-lauding, and over-resting your sense of God and self on what mere human beings promised to do.

Let's get specific. You've been playing your bitter story over and over again in your mind. As you do, you keep hardening your feelings and deepening the wound each time you relive the jagged facts. Now, you can do this for the rest of your life if you want. But play it out. What will you be in a decade or two or three? You will simply be a more cancerous soul, a less useful being—just another miserable creature known for whining about the church.

Yet here, right here, is where a turning can begin. Will you hold the biblical view of humanity up against your situation and see that people did what they did because they are flawed and sinful beings? No matter what harm they intended to do to you, can you reach behind it and take hold of the original cause: that we are all torn every day between the voice of demons and the image of God? That those who hurt you are playing out a bleak drama that is beyond your tale of woe? That they are trapped as surely as you are in this unbroken chain of bitter facts?

Then there is this: will you own that you got all mushy and dreamy-eyed and you forgot what monsters people can be? Will you at least consider not blaming them and admit for just a moment that your pain is partly your own fault? You forgot what you knew, forgot what your spirit was telling you, forgot that nothing in this world is perfect, even in church? So you are blaming others for your own over-believing, over-trusting, and over-reliance on what mere humans could do for your soul?

As you play your bitter story over again in your mind, you keep hardening your feelings and deepening the wound.

Trust me when I tell you that if you will allow this crack in the wall of your hatred and defense, it will lead to every other good thing that we hope to accomplish in the pages ahead. Ahead is rest for your anger-weary soul. Ahead, though you may not believe it now, is a Jesus kind of love for those you don't even trust. And ahead is peace, that feeling that happens when you come home to yourself again and find that God is already there.

CHAPTER 4

Lessons from a Season in Hell

I WANT TO ASK YOU TO DO A DIFFICULT THING. It will not be easy and it is so contrary to nature that you have likely never done it before.

I want you to take the most agonizing season of your life and examine it piece by piece. I want you to look again at those agonizing days of your wounding by the church and probe them carefully for the lessons you can learn. This will be something like an athlete watching the film of his game-losing mistake in painstaking slow motion again and again and again. It will take courage, and a brand of humility that defies embarrassment for the sake of gaining the wisdom that makes for a more meaningful life.

Let me tell you why I'm asking this. We human beings understandably run from pain. Anything that hurts sends us fleeing. And while this makes perfect sense when it comes to physical pain, we usually have the same urge to flee when it comes to emotional pain. This would make sense as well, except that with emotional pain we can only run from the cause, not the pain itself. If we sit on a sharp object, the pain stops when we jump up. When we are hurt emotionally, though, we carry the torment with us as we go.

But running from emotional pain is never a good idea, as it only leaves us damaged of soul and hindered in our ability to fulfill our purpose. We have to turn and face our torturous seasons and the scars they try to leave on our hearts.

Yet, I'm not just asking that you turn and face the pain. That would take courage enough. I'm asking something more. I want you to look at the kind of person you were while you were in the midst of the hurt. You see, we are meeting on these pages because you have gone through an experience that broke you, cut you open, and left you bleeding on the floor. What I am asking is that we look at who you were during that time you were raw and exposed and laid open so that we can find out what we need to know to heal and restore.

We often spout platitudes about how hard times make us better. What we should say is that hard times *can* make us better if we go through them in a redemptive way. Otherwise, hard times can just kill us, or crush our spirits so we are never whole again. But then, yes, hard times can lift us to new heights if we learn what we can about ourselves during those hard times and let these lessons lead us to a wiser, weightier life.

I'm reminded of an experience I had in the Syrian Desert. I was speaking with an Arab friend of how foreign the desert is to me and how—raised as an Army brat in Germany and now living in Tennessee—lush hills and flowing rivers are more to my liking. My friend took humorous offense and began extolling the glories of the "desert under God." Waving his arms in what I am sure were ancient ways, he said, "There is as much life in the desert as there is in the sea, but you must know where to find it!"

I cannot judge whether he was right about the physical desert because I have worked hard to spend as little time there as possible. I am sure, however, that he is right about spiritual deserts. In other words, during our dry and painful spiritual seasons, there is much life to be found, but we have to find it in places we have never considered before, digging for it in ways we have not yet tried.

Your horrific time of trouble offered you truths about yourself, windows into your own soul, and maps to the terrain of your inner life. Wise people learn to gather this intelligence to help them conquer themselves and then to live in loftier ways. Fools rush so quickly past their painful times and live so determined to never look back that they cannot hear wisdom calling to them. They usually end up living in constant cycles of folly and waste. It seems wise, then, that before we move on, we should slow down, face the crushing moments, and learn of ourselves what we may.

To make this as streamlined as possible and to give you a checklist that you can even invite others to help you use, I'm going to put this in the form of a series of questions.

Question #1: Of the things your critics said, what do you now know to be true?

You endured a bruising season. There were tensions and arguments and fights. In the time-honored way of most churches, there were likely meetings end upon end. And you heard things about yourself that stung. You may have refused them at the time, but they were nevertheless honest evaluations of who you are. Even if they were spoken by those who meant you harm. Still, they were truths spoken by those who knew you and it is essential that you ask yourself if there is wisdom to be found in those words.

The great missionary statesman E. Stanley Jones was known as the "Billy Graham of India" because he challenged Western ways of planting Christianity in Indian culture. He was controversial and his methods won him many critics, and this in turn forced him to ponder the impact of criticism upon his life. After years of reflection, he finally concluded that his critics were "the unpaid guardians of my soul."

Think about what this means, what it required of Jones. He first had to consider the possibility that truth can come even from those who opposed him. He looked into the criticism, separated the jewels of wisdom from the dung hill of empty words, and then applied that wisdom carefully to his life. Obviously, Jones had made this his habit and felt so grateful for the good it had done him that he was able to call his critics his "guardians," because they kept him from errors and excess, laziness and wrongheaded ideas.

It is a great art of living to be able to hear truth in the mouth of your enemies. Even those who hate you and mean to hurt you may still be right about what they see in your life. Though they shout their observations and probably intend them to wound you rather than help you, still they are giving you insight that can help you improve.

When I was leaving the pastorate in that horrible season that I've already described, words flew fast and furious as they tend to do at such times. During one particularly painful exchange, an elder turned to me and said, "You know, I've never felt important in your presence." Now this man certainly said this to wound me rather than help me be a better man, but what I learned from this barb was so valuable that I'm grateful for it to this day.

The church that I pastored had existed for eighty years before I got there, and the elders had long before won a reputation for being petty and small. My response to this was unwise. Essentially, my approach was summarized in the bumper sticker that says, "Lead, Follow, or Get Out of the Way." I thought the best approach to men of such character was to move fast and let them catch up. And the fact that the church grew dramatically during my time at the helm only fed my sense that this was the right way to go.

It is a great art of living to be able to hear truth in the mouth of your enemies.

I know now I was operating in pride. As I pondered that elder's words—that I had never made him feel important or needed—I realized that for the most part, these elders had been good men who wanted to team with me to change lives with the gospel of Jesus. They weren't the enemy and they might have been allies. Tragically, I saw them as foes bent on weighing me down and I did just about everything possible to keep them at a distance while insisting that they be impressed with what the staff and I were accomplishing.

What might we have done if we had truly been a team? What might we have been spared if I had surrendered my pride, submitted to their God-given role in my life, and welcomed their wisdom for my task? But since I did not, when that elder fired his bitter sentence at me like a bullet from a gun, I laughed it off as just another angry, meaningless assault. In the months that followed, though, I thought about what he said, first in anger, then in curiosity, and finally in understanding.

Ill-intentioned though it may have been, this criticism of me has changed the way I lead. There was truth in the mouth of my critic and he has, whether he wanted to or not, become the unpaid guardian of my soul. Thank you, Mr. Elder. And thank you, E. Stanley Jones.

Now, here is what you must do. If you are like me, you have spent many an hour replaying in your mind the verbal barbs that were lobbed your way. Let me assure you that this will do you no good. What you must do is stop replaying them and evaluate them instead. No matter the spirit in which they were said, is there truth in them for you? Did an enemy capture some insight into what about you must change? Is there anything you can apply to your life that will help you live more effectively for God?

Write down the core criticisms you have received. Take as long as you need to decide what in them is true and what in them is not. Then, throw away the barbs that were false and don't pick them up again. Remember, you've said such things about others, too. And on the matters that were true, pull those words into your life. Think about them. Pray about them. Run them by trusted friends. Put them in journals and let them become the instruments by which you navigate your life. In other words, let them change the way you conduct yourself in this world.

And do not forget to be grateful that even when hell was in session, God loved you enough to offer you wisdom for living your life.

Question #2: How did you try to medicate your wounded soul?

Every human soul is different. We are all shaped by both experience and design, by callings and the way our gifts mold our inner lives. Every soul has a bent, a drift, a way it wants to go. And when hard times come and the inner person writhes in torment, the soul reaches for what it thinks is anesthesia, for something to medicate the pain.

Usually what it wants is something artificial. Because your soul is part of the fallen, sinful creature that you are, it longs for a salve but seldom for permanent answers. It longs for pleasure rather than healing, a temporary peace rather than long-term righteousness. And so when we are facing times of thrashing agony, we try to meet our soul's need but often find that we are merely building bondages we will battle the rest our lives. The wise man takes note of this tendency of his soul, a tendency more pronounced in pain than in seasons of peace, and sets himself against these enemies of his inner life.

We have all seen the man who spins out of control and becomes a moral mess. He was the good father and the fine church member. He was respected on the job and a help to the community. But he gets fired or he goes through a divorce or angrily leaves his church over some offense. He becomes embittered and enraged and soon what once gave him moral restraint is no longer there. He excuses himself from the usual boundaries and starts seeking ease for his soul in places he never would before. He drinks or he eats to excess or he dips into porn or he becomes a raging, cussing mess. Perhaps he tries drugs or seeks his peace among prostitutes or becomes a violent man. Or it may be more subtle than that. He may dull his senses with hours of television or try to escape through extreme workouts.

What he has done is fulfill the warning of Jonah. This willful prophet was so offended at the mercy of God that he ran from his calling and ended up spending three days in the belly of a whale. When he realized his error, he prayed a prayer of repentance that concluded with this urgent warning for men of all time: "Those who cling to worthless idols forfeit the grace that could be theirs."[20]

And this is what we do. What we want and need in our bitter, rebellious times is God, but unwilling to turn fully to him, we reach for idols and forfeit his intended grace. Idols of pleasure. Idols of fantasy. Idols of vengeance and pride. We grasp these in hopes that they will ease our pain and show us the way out of our house of horrors. But since this is something only God can do, we simply end up building temples for the strongholds we will have to battle another day.

In my case, bitterness and rage kidnapped my gifts and nearly drove me insane. You see, I am a writer and a speaker: a man who works with words and crafts them for maximum impact. When I felt myself wronged and then descended into my own bitter spiral, I began spending hours preparing to set the record straight. I was going to blow everyone away, put my words together in just the right way so that they would realize how they had wronged me and cry out for forgiveness. I began walking my room for hours talking to them as though they were there. Oh, I reached Shakespearean heights! Man, I was good. My words would make a hardened jury weep. But one afternoon I realized that I had spent all day telling off an empty room. It was just me in my pajamas, telling men I would never see again why they were wrong. And I realized how pitiful I was. I felt ashamed. And more, I wondered if I had permanently left reality or if this was just a one-time visit to the land of the mentally infirm.

Words had become my drug. Pride and fantasy, the false answers for my soul. Other men might reach for french fries or *Playboy* or sports. I talked all day to people who weren't there, and worse, I was proud of how I moved those who heard. But no one did.

It was about this time that one of those pastors I mentioned took the time to hear me out and then leaned forward and lovingly said, "Shut up! Just, really, shut up! No, you don't understand. Don't talk. At all. Every time you open your mouth you deepen the pit. Just, please, don't say a word."

And over the months that followed I began to understand. Because I didn't drink to excess or eat mountains of food or frequent strip joints or plan the bombing of the choir loft, I thought I was free. But my addictions were just more socially acceptable and easily mistaken for my gifts. Thank God some tough pastors stuffed a sock in my mouth.

So here is what you need to do: You need to run your mind over that horrible season, the one that, in fact, you might still be in. You need to take pen in hand and write

Write down every way in which your soul has tried to artificially salve its own hurt or meet its own need. This is a list of the enemies of your soul.

down every way in which your soul has tried to artificially salve its own hurt or meet its own need. What results will be a list of the enemies of your soul. This will be valuable information. Whether you feel it or not, these are the idols that pull at your soul no matter your state, no matter the external peace you enjoy.

And once you've identified those enemies, you need to declare war. If you ate like a horse during your days of torment, make fasting and discipline part of your life. If you drank to excess or you toured the side streets of immorality, make sure those near you know; keep nothing close by you that feeds those desires. Repent before God, feed on the Scriptures that answer this drive, and give people the right to tackle you hard if you seem likely to stray.

You have been given a marvelous gift. You were cut open and left bleeding, and as painful as it was it gave you a chance to see what your inner Timmy reaches for that he ought not to have. Armed with this knowledge, you can truly live free.

Question #3: Were you clinging to anything that contributed to your church hurt?

The answer to this question is going to be harder for you than the others and here is why: we never want to take the blame. Even Scripture says that people always think their lives are blameless because we are descended from Adam. Remember him? He tried to blame his sins on his wife and God.

Adding to this tendency to refuse responsibility is the fact that we've been hurt and our hurt always triggers our "victim mode." The fog of our sense of injustice is so thick that we cannot see our actions for what they are. We edit the mental film of our deeds to fit the script that is in our heads, a script that frees us from responsibility no matter what reality is. It is always others who have done the misdeeds. We merely sat innocently by.

So having said this, let me ask again: were you clinging to anything that contributed to your church hurt? I can tell you that in my case I clung to several things that ultimately did me in. Again, I am Timmy on stun. First, the church I pastored had previously been pastored by an older man whom I saw as a father in the Lord. I stuck close to this man and tried to please him—even long after I knew I should go.

Second, this church was large and had a huge staff, many of them men near my age. Oh, how I needed that band of brothers. I love passionate men in pursuit of God. I love the sense of mission and the hard-hitting differences of opinion and the protective teaming when it all goes as it should. I imagine most everyone does. So, I stayed and I clung to that experience and I think I even inflated it in my mind, becoming blind to the dysfunctions I should have addressed.

Finally, I wanted to do good. I liked the size and the budget of this church and the opportunity it gave me to make a difference in the world. Though I knew I would not stay there forever, I stayed longer than I should have because I had things to do. I even had a list, you see, and my pride led me to believe that I could not leave until all I had in my heart to do was done.

So, like many of us, I did not pay attention to the voice of the Lord, to his ordering of my days and to the definition of his boundaries for that season of my life. I idolatrously grasped relationships and power and thus set myself up for the beating I took.

You may have figured out that I now spend a great deal of time helping people through their church hurts and consulting with churches in their difficult times. Almost every time I deal with people who have been harmed in a church or Christian organization, I can find something they have been clinging to that has kept them from moving on, something that jerked them out of season and into exposure to the barrage.

There was the Christian music star who frankly admitted that he stayed in a group long after he should have because of the money and the planes and the food. He wasn't trying to hide anything. He knew that his grasping ways had moved him out of godly positioning and into harm's way.

There was the pastor who had finished what he had set out to do when he took his church job but then it all became easy. His kids were out of college and the bills weren't that large anymore. There were the dinners out and that membership at the elite golf club. Why leave? Times were good. And then, you guessed it, his idolatry set him up for the bruising of his life when it all fell apart.

And there was that group of elders who thought they had the best pastor in the world. He could really preach and lead. Man, he was something. Oh, he had some moral flaws and, of course, his home life was a mess. But the offerings were huge and the people impressed. So they kept that man long after they should. In time, when the affairs and the "borrowing" of church funds came to light, the elders regretted their choice and had to let the man go. The next pastor, the one God had held in reserve all along, was more than they had ever dreamed, and in time they realized that they had clung to an idol and forfeited the grace that could have been theirs.

Before the knot of your pain and offense can be fully untied, you have to look your situation full in the face. What did you cling to that set you up for harm? What was the idol that held you fast long after you should have left? Where did the turn come when you got off the path of God's best?

These are hard questions but they are essential if you are going to get clean. And the answers will tell you what you must avoid in the days to come. For the likelihood is that you will find yourself in similar situations with similar options one day not too far down the road. But if you face your Timmy nature and deal with your sins now, you can easily pass the test and keep yourself from more bruising seasons of hell.

Question #4: What did those closest to you do when you went through the fire?

A man is known by the company he keeps. We all know that we can tell a great deal about people by looking at those they call friends. It is also true that we can tell a great deal about ourselves by what our friends do when we hit hard times.

I hope that during your seasons of suffering your friends stayed true. I hope they stood with you and encouraged you and helped you see the promise of a better day. I hope they were willing to step into the line of fire for you and that they spoke passionately in your defense as your critics railed. I hope that now, with the crisis past, you are able to share a wonderful meal with these same friends and tell war stories and laugh and deepen your commitment to each other with every word.

We can tell a great deal about ourselves by what our friends do when we hit hard times.

I hope this is so. I know, though, what crisis can do even to the dearest of friends. Some psychologists call it the "Oswald Complex." Several days after President John F. Kennedy was shot, just as the lead suspect in the assassination, Lee Harvey Oswald, was being taken from the Dallas police station, Jack Ruby ran up and shot him while he was handcuffed to two detectives. As they watched the films afterward, some psychologists noted that when Ruby approached Oswald with a gun, the two detectives actually pulled away rather than protect him from harm. And thus, the term Oswald Complex became a name for the natural tendency of people to pull away from those they have committed to defend when danger approaches.

I imagine you may have experienced this yourself. In fact, if you've gone through a humiliating season of public hardship, it almost is certain that you have. The accusations flew, you became a target, and your friends did not know what to do. Some believed the lies. Others just retreated into safety because they were unsure. Perhaps some of your own family members even stepped away from you or sided with those who meant you harm.

But there were some who were true, and how you love them for it. There may also be those you barely knew who stepped to your side—people you never would have expected to take such a stand. I want you to take note of all of this because in it you will find wisdom for your friendships in the future and an understanding of how people bond with you or perhaps don't.

What I needed to do when the dust settled after my painful season is what I'm asking you to do now: take a look at what kind of people you chose as friends, take a look at how you relate to your intimates, and then apply the insights you gain to your future relationships so you do not cycle through these same betrayals again.

I do not mean to be harsh, but I suspect that we have a tendency to choose friends unwisely. We befriend people because we have a common interest—say, golf or films—and we try to build a lasting relationship on that slim basis. Or we think people are close to us because we have a good laugh together and, gee, don't we all enjoy that little Mexican food joint on the corner? And when the crisis comes, we are shocked that they disappear, but we have to admit that we never asked any more of them than a little fun. Many of them were not friends in the first place; they were acquaintances. If we want friends, we have to look for something more.

I am moved by the story of Jonathan and David in 1 Samuel 18. After David killed Goliath, he gave an account to King Saul. And Jonathan, the king's son, looked on, seeing the Spirit on David and taking note that this was an exceptional man. Scripture tells us that "Jonathan became one in spirit with David, and he loved him as himself." Notice that the basis of Jonathan's devotion to David was his passion for God, his manly defense of the realm, his courage, and his willingness to sacrifice all for a cause.

We think people are close to us because we have a good laugh together. And when the crisis comes, we are shocked that they disappear.

We catch glimpses in the chapters that follow of what this friendship, this unselfish commitment, cost Jonathan. Saul descended into madness and a state of demon-possession, and in an unending jealous rage, he began to hunt David down. But Jonathan, whom we might naturally expect would want to curry favor with his father given the inheritance he was destined to receive, risked all to defend his friend. Jonathan warned David of his father's plans,[21] spoke well of David in the face of Saul's attacks,[22] served David in his time of crisis,[23] braved his father's spear in David's defense,[24] and repeatedly helped David "find strength in God."[25] Time and again, Jonathan renewed his covenant with David and finally, in sacrificial recognition of what God intended with David's life, he turned to his friend and said, "You will be king over Israel, and I will be second to you."[26] Though Jonathan was the heir apparent to the throne of Israel, he surrendered his rights in order to facilitate both God's plan and what was best for his friend.

Don't you love Jonathan for the spirit that was on him and for the devotion he gave to his friend? And don't you long for friends of the same kind? I do too, but I will tell you that you will only have a friend like Jonathan when you are first a Jonathan to the Davids in your life. In other words, if you long for a Jonathan/David relationship, you'll have to be a Jonathan first. This means that your friendships have to become about more than the game or the food or the late-night-yuk-it-up session. They must also be about destiny, about helping each other find strength in God, and about lifting each other to the high calling on your lives. Friendships of this quality are not likely to disappear when the humiliating season comes.

Take stock of your friendships. Look closely at those who abandoned you during the harsh times and then look at those who stayed. Who was fierce in love and devotion and who ran to protect themselves? Ask yourself why. Dig deep and find the keys to your own manner with friends. Then, make the changes you need to make. Become a Jonathan and you'll have Jonathans braving the spear of Saul in the next go-around.

Question #5: During the bruising season, what fed your inspiration and your dreams?

You are on the other side now. Whatever your condition of heart, you've endured, and now you are here. But if you look back to the days of the loneliness and the heartache, I'm betting you can remember moments that made the difference for you, times that filled you with purpose and with strength. This is what I want you to recapture now, for the very things that fed you when you were rising from the muck can also fuel you as you scale the heights of your calling. This is what I want you to know.

When I was in the darkest time of turmoil with my church, I read my Bible and I prayed by the hour. It made a difference, certainly, but I sensed I was unable to receive what I thought God was trying to give. I believe now he was trying to stoke a fire of heroic endurance in my soul though I was too bruised and angry to understand. So my loving God simply chose another way.

I spent more time in movies than usual during this time, and soon I realized that God was speaking to me from the screen. No, he didn't come down in a pillar of fire, but certain lines from films or quotes from documentaries echoed in my soul as though the words were destined just for me. I watched again a favorite movie, *Dead Poets Society*, and heard these words from a Walt Whitman poem: "That the powerful play goes on and you may contribute a verse." Oh, how I wanted simply to have a chance again to contribute a verse! Those words lifted me and stirred a determination in my inner being to endure the pain and play my role in history again.

I watched a documentary on Ernest Shackleton, the famous

explorer, and heard the narrator say, "It was a sad time; the kind that often befalls heroes." Though I did not think of myself as a hero, I realized at that moment that anyone who seeks to make a difference suffers on the way. Who was I to think I might be any different?

Sometimes it got silly. I walked past the open door of a room where the horror movie *Hellraiser* was playing. Though I have never seen the movie and don't like films of that kind, I heard someone in the film say, "Our scars remind us that our past was real," and immediately I knew that someday I would be helping people with the same wounds I had incurred. It made me that much more eager to survive my hardships while maintaining my character.

Then I happened to see a television news story about a female college basketball player. I noticed as the reporter interviewed the girl that her T-shirt bore the words, "Pain is weakness leaving the body." I knew then that I would be stronger one day for what I had endured.

I watched the movie *Patton* and was moved to tears by General Patton's sense of destiny and his belief that he had a role to play in history.

I turned on a movie and a Swahili proverb filled the screen:

Life has meaning only in the struggle,
Victory or defeat is in the hand of God,
So let us celebrate the struggle.

These words stirred me to fight on. And then, just as I thought my inner life was dying, I heard Albert Einstein say, "The tragedy of life is what dies inside a man while he lives." And I determined not to be yet another dead-of-soul, tragic man.

I can't tell you the difference these words made, though they came at odd times and sometimes from strange sources. By now you have probably noticed the pattern here. I am moved by history, by warriors, and by words that spring from contest and war. This is what reaches into who I am as both a man and as a Christian and stirs me to be my best. Encouraged by my pastor friends at the time, I took note of this and began steeping my soul in the themes that made me noble and fierce of faith and more passionate for God. I memorized the warrior passages of Scripture, read books on great men and women of the past, and devoured the works of gallant warriors down through time.

In other words, while I was in the pit, I learned what inspires my soul and then when I was free, I continued to stoke my inner fires in the same way. Again, the lessons from the suffering season have made the difference in my life ever since.

What about you? What was it that set you aflame, that made you determined to rise above? Don't be ashamed to name it. In my case it was history and words of great men as I found them in movies and books. For you it might be art or the truths found in science. You might be touched by different themes from history than I was, or it might be that fiction is your source or music or poetry. Your inspiration can come in many ways, but the art is to know it, to feed on it, and to let it propel you not just out of the pit but to the heights of your life.

Your inspiration can come in many ways, but the art is to know it, to feed on it, and to let it propel you to the heights of your life.

Take your time with this. Make long lists. Look over your journal or ask friends who walked with you at the time. Identify this important dynamic of your inner life and use it to help you live what you dream.

Although these are the five questions I want you to ponder, there may be other questions that are equally important for you. Perhaps some other essential questions for your life are "What was your view of God?" or "How did you spend your money?" or "What was the secret that you covered up to your destruction?" Whatever it is, you now know how to frame the question and you know that there is no sense in hiding from the truth. Facing the reality of that painful season when it felt as though you were in a sandstorm with no skin is the key to becoming whole now. So slow it down, take your time, and boldly dig into who you were at that time.

Believe me, you're going to need it for what's coming next.

CHAPTER 5

The Throne Room of Your Mind

THERE IS A SCENE THAT REPLAYS ITSELF again and again in my mind. Perhaps something like it appears on the screen of your mind as well. My version goes something like this:

I am seated in a large, ornate room. It is breathtakingly beautiful, with soaring pillars and stunning statuary. I am, for some reason, dressed in a toga and seated on a throne. In my left hand is a scepter and on my face is a look of nobility tempered with compassion and the wisdom of the ages.

I know, I know, but this is my fantasy so leave me alone!

The press is there. Walter Cronkite has come back to cover this scene and Larry King is perched at a desk nearby. I see Geraldo Rivera, microphone in hand, interviewing his way through the crowd, and Chris Matthews and Rush Limbaugh are heatedly discussing what is about to take place. Cameras are pressed tightly in an arc in front of me and all the networks are scurrying about in anticipation of the momentous event about to unfold.

Before me as I sit upon my throne, scepter in hand, is a line of people that extends all the way out the door and, I am told, even down the street. The people in this line are eager, many of them in tears. They press forward in their excited agitation and have to be urged to step back by the ushers, who are mountainous men on loan from the defensive line of the Tennessee Titans.

What has occasioned this historic moment is an event of global significance. You see, in an instant, everyone on earth who has ever wronged Stephen Mansfield has suddenly and dramatically become aware of his or her state. All of them, at the same time, wherever they were in the world, were suddenly stricken with the terrifying sense that I was right all along, that they have wronged me, and that they must immediately make amends. They have fallen to their knees or torn their clothes in agony or fallen on friends to weep out their grief. And then it struck them: "I must find Stephen. I must confess my wrongs."

From all over the world, then, the repentant have come. There is the friend who betrayed me and the coach who didn't understand. My fifth grade teacher is making her way forward as is the girlfriend who dumped me for that geeky guy in eleventh grade. The press is reporting that on long flights from Asia and trains from New York, in van loads from Tulsa and by the truckful from Abilene, weeping, agonized people are making their way to where I now am—in my toga, on my throne, scepter in hand.

And so they come before me, one by one. When their turn comes in the line, they drop to their knees, bedraggled and tear-stained as they are. They take the hem of my garment and, between heart-rending sobs, they tell me of how they have wronged me and how sorry they truly are. Now, they affirm, they will go forth in the way of righteousness, a way that I have shown them, and they will never again offend.

The scene gets blurry at this point. I think I say some words of astonishing insight and extend my scepter. I can't really recall. But whatever I do, the effect on the people in line is transforming. Beams of light strike their faces and as they rise, they whisper to each other of what it is like to be in my presence and of how I was right all along. If only they had listened.

And the line moves forward, one tortured soul at a time, and I—my face tender and wise—extend mercy to each one and send them forth into the world to live lives transformed by my grace.

This scene plays itself over and over again in my mind and gives me comfort as I think of it. It is a wish, a dream, a prayer. It is my final fantasy that one day they will all come: the teacher who told my mother in front of me that I was "immature and retarded" and the kid who blackened my eye in second grade and, yes, the pastor who lied about me to save his job. They will all come, my fantasy assures me, if I will but wait until that destined day.

And you, my friend, may have a similar image playing in your head. Perhaps it is in a different setting and you aren't wearing a toga and it is likely the whole scepter thing seems a bit too weird. But if you are human and have ever been hurt, you probably have a scene not too unlike mine.

So hear me on this like your life depends on it: *It ain't ever gonna happen!*

Never. Not in this life or any other.

Say it out loud to yourself: *It ain't ever gonna happen!*

Go find your spouse or roommate or friend and announce it like the house is on fire: *This ain't ever gonna happen!*

I say this because we should laugh at our folly together. Our secret is out. In those inner, private temples of our hearts we have been nursing a hope that one day something like this would occur. There would be that moment of reckoning, that day of finally setting it straight. They would hear you defend yourself with perfect clarity and then, struck by the brilliance of your defense, they would fall before you in repentant agony. And so it would go. But never, ever will this take place. We can rehearse our case in the mirror all we want. We can drive down the road telling our steering wheel how things will one day be. We can pace our room proclaiming our truth with skill to match the great speeches of all time. But it will all be in vain.

People move on. People forget. And people die. Go on, admit it: some of the people you are making your secret case to—you know, those people you hope will be in that line in your throne room—some of those people are dead, for heaven's sake. And in our pitiful human need to be justified, we are still waiting for the day when they will tell us we were right and they were wrong so that now all can be good with the universe.

The problem with carrying this inner hope—even if it doesn't take the ridiculous form my fantasy does—is what it is doing to us in the meantime, while we carry it around unfulfilled. You see, the very fact that we have this desire for justification is a sign that we feel there is a debt to be paid. Someone, somewhere needs to pay us what we are due, though in this case it isn't money: it is apologies and acknowledgments and tributes to our wounded ego. And the horrible truth is that the very desire we carry for those who have wronged us to pay their debt is the sign that we haven't forgiven them. You see, as we'll discuss in the pages ahead, forgiveness is the releasing of debt. So my little fantasy is a grievous indication that I have not forgiven others and this is the worst news of all, for it means that I am in a prison of my own making.

I will explain this more fully soon, but first let's spend some more time exploring what it means to be in an unforgiving state. The Bible uses the word *offended* to describe the condition of someone who believes themselves wronged. When people are offended, they believe they have been wounded or damaged by another's actions. They walk around with a constant sense that someone has sinned against them and has an obligation to put it right. To say it another way, to be offended is to live in an incomplete state, waiting for one who has wounded you to make things right. This isn't necessarily good news, for among the promises the Bible makes is that offenses will come. In other words, they are part of life in this world. Much that distinguishes maturity from immaturity—and happiness from misery—is how you respond to the offenses that life insists on dealing out to us all.

Knowing this, we might be tempted to walk around feeling like victims. After all, we have to live in this fallen world and since the Bible tells us that offenses are going to come hard and fast in this life, what choice do we have? We are destined to endure hurts or wounds that rain down on us like a meteor shower and there is really nothing we can do about it, right?

No. The truth is less bleak and more liberating than that. Take a breath and settle in and see if what follows doesn't help.

There is some tremendous wisdom to be found in the original word that is used in the New Testament for the word *offense*. You see, we naturally read the Bible in the English language, but the New Testament wasn't originally written in English. It was written in a form of Greek called Koine, and we should be glad it was. Koine Greek is a marvelously expressive language. It offers us word pictures that the Holy Spirit chose to use in communicating New Testament truth. These pictures can carry deep and transforming meaning for our lives.

For example, we see the word *sin* in the New Testament and we think it just means a wrong we commit before God. But the Greek word for sin is an archery term that means "to fall short of the target." In other words, you shoot the arrow, you don't have enough power, and your arrow falls on the ground short of the target. Isn't this a much more vivid and encouraging picture? Or take the word *comforter* that is used of the Holy Spirit. Our modern word *comforter* just conjures up the idea of a person who makes us feel better after we have suffered. But the Koine Greek word for *comforter* actually means "one called alongside to help." It is an image that comes from the long distance races of the Greek Olympic Games. In the last miles of a race, a runner could appoint someone to run beside him and encourage him, point out challenges on the road, and help him set his pace. This word used to describe this fellow runner was—you guessed it—the same Greek word used for the Holy Spirit's role in our lives. What a great image!

There is a marvelous picture from the Koine Greek that helps us understand what it means to be offended, as well. This word keeps me from thinking I am the victim of offenses and instead shows me what I can do about them. It's the word *scandalon*. Yes, we get our word *scandal* from it, but that isn't the most important connection for us now. The Holy Spirit chose this word, I believe, because it has a very specific application for the healing of our souls.

The Greek word *scandalon* refers to a very specific part of an animal trap. Can you picture in your mind a bear trap? It is a round device with jagged metal teeth. If you have spent a good portion of your life watching cartoons, you may remember that this is the kind of trap that Wile E. Coyote often set for the Road Runner. It is a round trap that you snap open and then set the bait in the middle on a small plate. You'll want to choose smelly stuff that draws the animal and makes him stick his nose or his paw into the trap. Since the trap is anchored to a tree or a large rock, once the animal takes the bait and the trap closes, he is caught and cannot get away. Either he dies of his wounds or the trappers kill him when they return.

> Much that distinguishes maturity from immaturity— and happiness from misery— is how you respond to the offenses that life insists on dealing out to us all.

Well, the small plate in the middle of the trap is called the *scandalon*. Think about this. Is the Holy Spirit telling us something by this choice of words? Sure he is. When we are offended, we are taking the bait of a trap that has been set for us.

Let's think this through. You get hurt or angered by a situation in your life. In your pain, you reach for the bait that is set on the plate, the *scandalon*, in the middle of that trap of offense. In other words, you give yourself to all the raging feelings that come from your wounding. The moment you do this, the moment you touch that plate, the trap snaps shut. You are caught.

Paul's words in 2 Timothy 2:24-26 confirm this idea that offenses are actually traps intended to capture us:

> *And the Lord's servant must not quarrel; instead, he must be kind to everyone, able to teach, not resentful. Those who oppose him he must gently instruct, in the hope that God will grant them repentance leading them to a knowledge of the truth, and that they will come to their senses and escape from the* trap of the devil, *who has taken them captive to do his will.* (emphasis mine)

This is a critically important truth for us and it is essential to helping us heal from our church wounds. In all of our angry mediations and rehearsing of the situation, we have viewed the offense as something that happened *to us*, something that others did. This has made us passive, recipients of wrongdoing who are without any remedy, without any power to make a change. It is like being told that you have a disease and that now you must simply lay back and let the doctors work. You must be passive in the face of your disease.

But being offended is not like this. The Holy Spirit is trying to tell us with this word picture that as horrible as the circumstances of our offense have been, we nevertheless made a choice in those circumstances to take the bait of offense. And that is the point. We had a choice. We weren't passive in the process. And if we had a choice to take the bait, we can also exercise our choice to get out of the trap. Understanding this critical point is the beginning of being free.

There is an image I would like for you to carry in your mind. It comes from combining the words of 2 Timothy 2:24-26 with the Greek word *scandalon*. Paul tells us in his words to Timothy that when we are offended and in strife, we have taken the bait of a trap that the devil has set for us. If we see this in terms of that bear trap image, we can imagine the devil laying bear traps of offense along the path of our lives.

In fact, do that now: picture your life as a long road along which the devil has placed big round, jagged-toothed bear traps. They will always dot your path and you will always have a choice as to whether you step into those traps or avoid them. Carry this image in your head as a warning and as a picture of the biblical truth that "offenses will come."

But let's take it one step further. If the devil is indeed setting traps for you—you in particular rather than believers in general—then ask yourself what bait he might use for you. In other words, if you were the devil, how would you trap you? If you will give this some thought, you will probably arrive at some keys to avoid taking the bait of offense in the future.

For example, I have already figured out that the bait of betrayal works with me. I love loyalty and that sense of belonging to a tribe that we are all made for. Betray me, set me up with friendship and then dump me for another, or hurt me on purpose, and I will want to hate you. I'm not saying this is right, I'm just saying that I have learned that betrayal draws me into the trap of offense. Knowing this, I can watch for it. I can use this information as military intelligence in my personal battle against the devil's schemes and my own sinful nature.

What about you? What bait is most effective in drawing you into offense, strife, and bitterness? What is it that immediately wounds you or makes you angry or makes you hate or makes you want to strike back at another? Is it injustice? Is it someone insulting your intelligence? Is it a racist attitude or someone messing with your money or somebody being cruel to one you love? There are infinite varieties of bait, but you need to identify the exact bait that draws you into the trap of offense.

What is it that immediately wounds you or makes you want to strike back at another?

Again, picture your life strewn with these traps and set with the bait that you now realize works for you. You don't have to take the bait that is set on these traps. You can simply avoid them. But you will always be tempted and you need to know this. The devil is trying to shape your life with wounding and offense in order to keep you from a life defined by the purposes of God. These traps of offense are his primary tools. Don't be caught off guard. See these traps for what they are and learn to avoid them.

In light of this biblical picture of offense, look back at your painful episode with the church. Were there traps set for you in that situation? In fact, look back over your life and see if you haven't been taking the bait on traps of offense for the whole course of your life. Some people have seldom been offended and don't find that bitterness is much of a factor in their lives. Others find that the whole path of their lives has been determined by situations of strife and wounding, which indicates that they have been defined by the devil's traps more than by any sense of calling or destiny. Hold on to this thought and we'll talk about it more in the pages to come.

Now that we realize that we are in an unforgiving state, that we have taken the bait of a trap set by the devil, and that we are deeply offended—particularly if we are waiting for that silly throne room experience—let's look at what that offended state is doing to us.

In Hebrews 12:15, we read these words: "See to it that no one misses the grace of God and that no bitter root grows up to cause trouble and defile many." There are two Greek words used here that help us add to our picture of what it means to be offended. The word *bitter* comes from the Greek word *pikros*, which means "to cut or to prick" or to be "pointed or sharp . . . pungent." The Greek word for defile is *miano*, which means "to stain or dye with a color." The author of Hebrews is telling us that we should not allow the sharp, bilious nature of bitterness to defile or "color" us. In other words, don't let the poison of bitterness infect you.

I have merged these words in my mind with that powerful image of the bear trap that we've been talking about. If I had any artistic ability at all, I would draw a picture of that bear trap—but I would draw it not with jagged metal teeth but with syringes instead. Inside these syringes would be the poison of bitterness.

Take a moment and think about this question: Have you ever known a man so eaten up with bitterness that nearly everything he said or did was permeated by a sharp, angry, bitter edge? He's the kind of man that can't even ask you to pass the salt at dinner without leaking out a bitterness or a sourness that all could feel. You want to take a shower after spending time with him. He may not even realize it, but his spirit is so tainted by the poison of bitterness that it flows out into all he says and does. People avoid him because of it, and perhaps you are even tempted to get out of the way when you see him coming. At some time in his life, this man stepped into the trap of offense, and bitterness has been flowing through his veins ever since. He is defiled and tainted—or "colored"—by the acidic poison in his soul.

This is what it means to be offended and to be in that unforgiving state. You sustain a blow and it hurts—deeply. Someone betrayed you or lied about you or hurt your feelings or humiliated you. And so you respond, not with love and forgiveness, but with hate and vengeance and bitterness. You have taken the bait and now the trap is closed. The more you rehearse the wrongs against you and the more you stay in that trap, the more the syringes of bitterness release their toxins into your soul. You become increasingly bitter, increasingly sour, and the poison spreads out to taint all you do. You are defiled—and miserable.

Yet this may not be the worst of it. I want you to remember the last words of that passage we read in 2 Timothy 2:24-26. It says that the trap of offense is designed by the devil, "who has taken them captive to do his will." Clearly, the trap of offense is not designed just to damage you. It is designed to take you captive so that you in turn can be used by the devil to damage others. In other words, the devil wants to call you into his ministry, and he uses the strife and bitterness that is working through your soul when you are offended.

Let me explain this using an image from Ephesians 4:26-27. Paul tells us, "In your anger do not sin: Do not let the sun go down while you are still angry, and do not give the devil a foothold." The Greek word for *foothold* is *topos*. We get our words *topography* or *topographical* from it. It means territory or, sometimes, strategic territory. Paul is saying that when we are unrepentantly angry, we give the devil access to strategic territory in our lives. Our usual Christian word for this is *stronghold*.

When I was teaching this concept to my church, I often asked for help from a man in the audience. I would look for a guy who was larger than I am and have him join me on stage. I would then tell the audience that even though this man was bigger than I am and could perhaps take me in a fair fight, I could control him if I had a "strategic hold." Then, I would turn the man's back toward me and grab him by the belt. Often I would have more than just his belt in my hand, which sent the audience into hysterics. Yet I would demonstrate how just by gaining a firm grip on the man's belt from behind, I could pretty much control him. In fact, this hold is so effective that police use it all the time. This is a perfect illustration of a "stronghold," or that strategic territory in our lives to which the devil has access when we give ourselves to anger and bitterness. In fact, most any sin that we leave unconfessed and untreated can open the door to a stronghold of evil.

> *Most any sin that we leave unconfessed and untreated can open the door to a stronghold of evil.*

There is a pattern here and we have all seen it. Perhaps we have been caught in it ourselves. A person is wounded by the actions of others—in our case, his church—and that wound is nasty and deep. Rather than respond with forgiveness and peace, the offended person nurses the wound and makes it worse by replaying it in his mind and plotting his revenge. He has taken the bait and is in the trap of offense. Now those syringes of bitter liquid are being emptied into that already wounded soul. And here is where the dark plan begins to unfold, for the devil's design was not just to capture that one person, but to use him to bring others into the bitter fold. So now, this embittered, angry, wounded being goes about offending others: cussing them out, being impatient, being harsh at home, spilling his bitter stories out on his friends and their children. He goes into the ministry—a ministry of bitterness and offense.

And you have been in his congregation. At the coffee shop or the bar, at the party or the restaurant, you have inadvertently brought up his church or his pastor, or perhaps a friend he once had or even his father. And in an instant, you could feel the change. The stronghold of anger and sour rage kicked in and you were caught in the blast. It was like a blowtorch. In fact, his voice may even have changed and his face contorted to something almost unrecognizable. That stronghold was in control. Was he demon possessed? No, not necessarily. But he has yielded control to that poison in his soul and unwittingly tried to draw you in as well.

"Be angry and bitter as I am," he was saying, whether he knew it or not. "Go ahead. It feels good. That rage keeps you warm, that bitterness makes all things possible. There are no restrictions on your actions or your words here in the Land of the Leaking Wounded. C'mon. We call this being free."

But of course he is not free. And if you watched him over time, you would find that every arena of his life is in decline. I tell you that this is true not only from my own experience but from years of helping the bitterly wounded recover themselves again. You can almost graph the decline on a chart. Their marriages, their relationships with their children, their friendships—all suffered. This is because their unforgiving, hardened hearts have become distant from God and from the moral vision to which they had committed their lives. They eat or drink or party or entertain themselves nearly to death. Nothing is to be denied them, after all. Their bitterness becomes their license for excess. And so they sink, as captives of the devil and taking still other captives as they go.

But what is the solution? The solution is to forgive, to let go of the bait in that trap and pull yourself free. The solution is to recover your soul from the pit. Yet, before we turn in that direction, I want you to hold your life up against the pictures we have seen in these words. I want you to locate yourself first. Look hard at the church hurt you have sustained and the way it came about. There was the wound, yes, but there was also the choice you had at that moment. You could have forgiven and understood—and then moved on with your life: a clean heart, perhaps in another church or perhaps making it work where you were. But instead you took the bait. You have to see this. You took the bait you did not have to take. You *chose* to be angry and bitter and small. You spent hours telling others of the wrongs they did to you and you probably medicated your pain with something unclean, as we've seen. And all the while, those syringes of bitterness were spreading the infection in your soul.

Now, all this time later, you know the devil has you in his hold. No, you aren't living out a scene from *The Exorcist.* Your head doesn't spin around and you don't projectile vomit and you aren't saying the Lord's Prayer backward in Latin. But you know something has moved in. You feel a strength behind the evil that draws you and images come into your head that you know didn't arise on their own.

And what's more, you could make a list of the people that this bitter flow through your life has affected. You have either called together a band of disciples of your own or you have slammed into others, leaving them wounded and spinning out of control. You have to see this. It is a normal pattern of the wounded and of those infected of soul. And only by seeing it and acknowledging it as true can you ever turn and once again become whole.

I've told you from the beginning of this book that I would be tough with you, that I was your coach and not your loyal fan. Here is where it leads us. And let me make this clear: there is nothing that happened in that wounding experience with that church that is worth what is happening to you now.

It is time to make a change. And that change begins with forgiving.

If you have attended a church for any time at all, you've probably heard sermons on forgiving others. You may have even been moved by them, and when they were done you held the list of your least favorite people before God and tried to let go of your offense. You prayed the prayers that the pastor taught you and you called people to apologize for your anger and you tried to make amends. Perhaps it worked for you and you walked out free. Or perhaps no breakthrough came and you found yourself once again chipping away at the iceberg of your soul and hoping for warmer days.

I grew to hate sermons on forgiveness, even my own. They convicted me, true, and I did the things I was asked to do to deal with my offense and my hurt. But it seldom worked and I soon came to understand that there was a stronghold in my soul. It seemed as though my inner life was coated with Velcro that trapped hurt and offense and held it tight. Though I thought of myself as a fairly loving person, I could never let the impact of being wronged go. I fed it. I fantasized about it. I even used it to fuel my intensity in sports or my efforts to rise in the world. Because I could not let what offended me go, I used it as fuel and this only caused it to attach more firmly to that Velcro of my soul.

Forgiving came hard for me and the tra-ditional sermons didn't help. It wasn't until I began to press into the matter on my own, crying out to God to save me in my pitifully hardened state, that I found some keys that have set me free. Let's apply them to your heart and see if they won't help.

It is time to make a change. And that change begins with forgiving.

I've come to believe that the reason most sermons on forgiveness didn't work for me is that they appealed to sentiment and emotions first of all. They wanted me to feel differently about the people who had wronged me and then to act sweetly and lovingly toward them based on those new feelings. But those new feelings never came. I listened to the pastor's words. I really did. And I tried to manufac-ture new feelings, straining like a chicken squeezing out an egg, but nothing happened. And I would walk out of church at the conclu-sion of yet another sermon on forgiveness knowing that nothing real had taken place.

What I needed were actual steps to take, things to do that would ultimately leave me changed. I didn't find these in most of the ser-mons I heard. I did find them, however, as I paid attention to the words God used for forgiveness in Scripture. Building my approach to forgiveness on these words was the beginning of cleaning out the toxins in my soul.

There are three words used for forgiveness in the New Testament: *aphiemi*, *aphesis*, and *charizomai*. Each presents a distinct facet of what forgiveness is and each of these facets is essential to being set free.

Aphiemi (pronounced "a-fee-me") means "to send away or to set free" and it should invoke in our minds a very powerful Old Testament image. You see, when we read the words of the New Testament, the spirit and imagery of the Old Testament should always loom just behind. In other words, we should not read the New Testament as though all the Old Testament is passed away, but rather we should read the New Testament as though it is overlaid on Old Testament truth. Some scholars have called the New Testament a commentary on the Old Testament and though this is not literally true, it does show us how tight the connection between the two ought to be. So when we see the word *aphiemi* and know that it means "to send away or to set free"—particularly when we are talking about forgiving sins—a definite image from the pages of the Old Testament ought to arise in our minds: the image of the scapegoat.

You may recall that in Leviticus 16, God told Moses that on the Day of Atonement a scapegoat was to be chosen. This meant that a goat was chosen by casting lots and then that goat was brought to Aaron, the High Priest. Aaron was to "lay both hands on the head of the live goat and confess over it all the wickedness and rebellion of the Israelites—all their sins."[27] The goat was then carried to a solitary place and released into the desert, carrying with it all the sins of the people.

Once I understood this, it helped me forgive. First, I came to understand that Jesus is the scapegoat for a New Testament people and that he had taken upon himself the wrongs and the sins of the people who had harmed me. If I was going to "send away" the sins

people had committed against me—as the word *aphiemi* suggests—
then I would have to place those sins on Jesus just as Aaron did and
then send those sins away. It helped me to take this literally. I made
an actual list of the sins people had committed against me and then I
did what Aaron did: I spoke those sins onto Jesus. If Bob had stolen
something from me, I prayed "Lord, I understand that you love Bob
and you died for his sins. I put Bob's sin of stealing on you, knowing
that you have forgiven Bob and died to atone for that sin." I did this
for every sin I had been stewing about.

It made a difference not only because the Holy Spirit was lifting the imprint of each of these sins from my heart as I prayed, but
because the sins and hurt had somewhere to go. I know this sounds
odd, but in all the sermons I had ever heard about forgiveness, I
was simply asked to feel differently about someone's wrongs. Now
I was sending those wrongs away from me and onto the ultimate
sacrificial goat, Jesus, who dissolved those sins by his blood and by
his love. This was more than a mind game: it was real spiritual business. Perhaps because I am a male and perhaps because I am an ener-
getic "action" kind of guy, having a process that discarded the wrongs
against me rather than just sitting around trying to manage my feelings made the power of forgiveness real.

There was a second benefit to this compelling image for me
and it was the defense it gave me when hurt and accusation came
back around. This always happens, you see. Both because we are by
nature a grudge-keeping people and because our enemy wants to
keep us small and bleeding as the memories of the wrongs we have
endured and the feelings that come from our wounds try to take
up residence again in our souls. If forgiveness is nothing more than

a rearranging of our feelings, we have no defense against this. But if forgiveness is a formal process of sending sins and wrongs away from us and placing them upon Jesus on the cross, we have a barrier between us and the darkness that tries to come back in. I have often found myself saying aloud as some accusing, angry image formed in my head, "No. I've sent that away. Both that man and I are free. Jesus, the scapegoat, has taken that for us both." And the image goes away. This is more than just self-talk and more than games with images in my head. This is spiritual reality and the fruit of it in my life is beyond any doubt.

In a moment I will want you to do the "sending away" that I have done and that the Bible describes, but for now, let's strengthen our resolve with another image from New Testament Greek. The second word that means forgiveness is *aphesis*, and it means "to release, as from prison."

This single word began to have astonishing power for me when I came to understand that I had built a trophy room among the chambers of my heart. This trophy room was a spacious place lined with shelves, and on each shelf were little cages. Each of these cages housed someone who had wronged me. There—second from the left on the third shelf up—was that same fifth grade teacher who told my mother in front of me that I was "immature and retarded." Oh yes, and on that second shelf down, somewhere in the middle, was Coach Madison. Yeah, I remember him. I used to get an imaginary stick and poke him through the bars of that cage. And there is that elder in the big cage on the left. This is the guy who stirred up most of the lies against me. I loved to take his cage in my hands and shake it a bit, just to watch that elder flop around.

None of this was real, of course, but this was the image I had in my mind. And when I wanted to feel better about myself or feel justified in my hate, I would go into that trophy room to remember what horrible things these folks had done. Oh, it was nice to feel so superior and so right about who I was. And I could lecture them aloud—because of course they couldn't talk back—assuring them that their suffering in those cages would never end.

It was all so convenient and confirming until something happened. I came across the word *aphesis*. It taught me that to forgive is "to release, as from prison" and this made me aware that my trophy room might be under siege. Clearly, this word meant that if I was going to truly forgive, I had to let the folks in my trophy room go free. But it got worse. I read Matthew 6:14-15. What a bummer.

It says, "For if you forgive men when they sin against you, your heavenly Father will also forgive you. But if you do not forgive men their sins, your Father will not forgive your sins."

I stood up from this verse and stepped into my trophy room. I had worked so hard to create it and I loved it. But this time when I stepped inside, I realized something I hadn't before. I look up through the ceiling and I saw that my little trophy room was actually within an even larger prison. You see, God had said that if I did not release those who have wronged me from the prison where I had them bound, he would not release me. So as long as I kept people chained in my beloved little trophy room, God held me bound in a larger prison of my own construction as well. That scared me, and I knew what I had to do. After a heartfelt prayer of repentance, I went into my room and opened up each cage. I told them they were all free and that I forgave them. And I asked them to forgive me. Then

I roasted weenies on the bonfire that came from burning my trophy room down.

We all have our own trophy rooms. These are the places in our minds where we revisit the episodes of offense in our lives and rekindle the fires of anger against those who've treated us badly. We use our trophy rooms to justify our rage and to set ourselves at a distance from the people we ought to love. We use them to feel better about ourselves and excuse ourselves from the commands of God. But our trophy rooms are built right in the center of the Penitentiary of God and it is actually we who are in bondage. God will not free us until we free others. So it is time to let them go. Your father, that friend, the former wife or husband, and that church that ripped you up inside? It is time to let them go. Open the cages, tell them you're sorry, forgive them as Jesus forgave you, and burn that trophy room to the ground.

The image of the scapegoat and the knowledge that my trophy room only imprisoned me made a huge difference in my efforts to forgive. But this last word of the three is what really set me free. The third word used in the New Testament for forgiveness is *charizomai*. It means "to bestow a favor or extend mercy."

In my journey to forgive, I came to realize that I had a tendency to transform my mental image of those who wronged me. It couldn't just be that a friend made a mistake and dealt out a little hurt. I wouldn't just leave it that an elder handled something clumsily but really wasn't a bad guy. Oh, no. Those who wronged me had to be tools of the Prince of Darkness. Everyone who did me harm was demon possessed and in blood-covenant league with the Antichrist. In other words, if someone hurt me, I concluded that the hurt was intentional, that it was a self-conscious evil on the other person's part, and that the minions of Satan were surely involved. This was pride, of course—the belief that anything that hurt me had to be part of some galactic conspiracy against me personally—and it did not make forgiving any easier.

What I was missing in my pride and my need to inflate all wrongs against me was what I have come to understand as the essential key of forgiveness. I call it the hook of compassion. When I look at those I want to forgive, I strive to not see them in evil terms, but to find the compassionate narrative behind their hurtful actions against me.

We all have places in our minds where we revisit the episodes of offense in our lives and rekindle the fires of anger against those who've treated us badly.

Here is how it works. You want to forgive your father. You know that your anger and your hurt have done you no good and you want to be set free. But he was horrible, wasn't he? He was harsh and cutting and mean. He was too rough in discipline and too distant from your world and too demanding in every arena of your life. You can hardly remember a tender conversation or a meaningful expression of love. And you've hated him because of it. Now, you want to be free. So find the hook of compassion. Start with what you can be grateful for. You never lacked for food or clothing and he was always good to your mother. He was home every evening and, given the perversions that have haunted our generation, it never even crossed your mind that he might come to your room at night for something impure. He was honest and respected at work and he loved you in his own way. And when you look at his parents you realize that he was never going to be a television dad, that he was never nurtured in that way. He did the best he could do. That's really it, isn't it? He did the best he could do. And if you can start with this and realize that much of your offense comes from your bloated expectations, you can be grateful for the good that he did and start to forgive him for what he can never be.

The same might be true of, let's say, a pastor. Perhaps your pastor hurt you. He mentioned you harshly in a sermon or he disciplined you in a public and humiliating way. Or maybe he neglected you and left you exposed when he could have stepped in and helped you. Whatever his misdeeds, you've pushed away. You've left the church but now you have to fight the hatred and the pain. It's tainting you and you know you have to forgive.

Find the hook of compassion. Enter this pastor's narrative. Perhaps he did do wrong but to see him as evil or as a false shepherd or as an emissary of darkness won't do you any good. Perhaps you can see him as the slave of a bad theology that makes him think he has to correct his members publicly and during a Sunday morning service. Perhaps you can realize he's under tremendous pressure, that he has more than a few troubles at home, and that he is insecure about his job and compensates by being overly bold. Maybe you can try to remember the good he has done and be open to the possibility that he knows he did wrong and wishes he could take it back.

It may even be that you can find absolutely nothing redeeming about the people who have wronged you. Perhaps the only hook of compassion you can find is to pity them in their sinful state. Whatever the case, if you can find even the smallest opening of compassion for their lives, that *charizomai* spirit of mercy and grace can flow in. Forgiveness can reign and you will be free.

Now let us put all this together. It is time to take stock. We have talked about what being offended can do to us, how we take the bait of a trap that then becomes a stronghold in our lives. We have seen how that stronghold presses poison into our hearts and pollutes our spirits so that we in turn taint others through our unclean and wounded ways.

> *If you can find even the smallest opening of compassion for their lives, that* charizomai *spirit of mercy and grace can flow in. Forgiveness can reign and you will be free.*

I want you to review the description of this downward progression as I offered it at the beginning of this chapter. Take some time, pull aside, and hold these words up against your life. You may need to make a list of the ways in which you see yourself fulfilling the biblical description of an offended and trapped man. Or you may need to sit with friends, asking them to read these words too, and then let them hold up a mirror to your life. In other words, I want you to see the truth. Perhaps not everything I've described applies to you, but you must honestly confront and decide to own whatever does apply.

Journal it. Make lists. Pray out loud and ask God to shine a light on what you cannot see. And take your time. This is important. You have come to these pages because you want to be set free, because you know you are not whole. Find yourself in this mirror of truth and refuse to forget what you see, no matter how disturbing.

And once you have fully confronted your bitter and ensnared state, let's move on with the business of forgiving. As you think about the three Greek words we looked at, perhaps one of them held a specific truth for you that resonated in your heart. Walk through that door. If the image of the trophy room and the prison you are in is what most stirs you to make a change, go with it. Or perhaps it is the image of the scapegoat or the hook of compassion that enflames your heart and gives you some hope. Whatever the draw, go before God and ask him to help you to forgive. Tell him you see what you've done and you are going to set the captives free. Then do what we've discussed: send the sin away, free the captives from your bitterness and your hate, and extend the mercy that comes from entering the story of those who've wronged you. There is no formula. Now that you know what forgiveness looks like—that it is arriving at a point where there is no debt, where all the wrongs against you are sent away and dissolved in Jesus' blood—you can ask the Holy Spirit to help you find your own way out.

Don't for a minute think that I am telling you this is easy. Don't think that this came easily for me and that now I'm speaking down to you. I'll confess to you that I failed so many times that I finally had to go at it another way. I actually made an enemies list. I know, I know: it all sounds very sinister and small. Still, I worked so hard at forgiving and found so little change that I finally decided to simply make a list of all those whose actions still lived in my memory as a source of bitterness and pain.

I had read Matthew 5:43-45, which says, "You have heard that it was said, 'Love your neighbor and hate your enemy.' But I tell you: Love your enemies and pray for those who persecute you, that you may be sons of your Father in heaven." In Luke 6:28, Jesus adds these words: "Bless those who curse you." I realized that I was having no success forgiving in the usual way. I was so convinced that certain folks had specifically tried to harm me that I could not pray and confess myself into a loving attitude of heart. So I just gave up and acknowledged these folks as my enemies. But then I was bound by what God commands me to do to my enemies: love them, pray for them, and bless them.

Knowing that I was in a real crisis of heart and needing to take extreme measures, I fulfilled these words literally. I made a list of those I deemed my enemies. Then, every day, I held their names before God, prayed for them, and blessed them—meaning that I spoke positive words from Scripture over their lives. I did this for months, and just when I was wondering if it was making any difference, a friend told me that one of these enemies had cancer and was soon to die. I immediately burst into tears. Though I would have labeled this man an enemy months before, my hours of praying for him and blessing him and trying to love him had brought about a change. True, I was not where I wanted to be in forgiving this man, but I also was not as I had been: wishing only harm would come to his life.

It was the beginning of forgiveness, and as time went on, I softened. I began to find compassion for these people and it became a bit easier to let them out of my trophy room and send their sins away. In other words, biblical forgiveness became possible. And the biggest change was in me. My passion for God slowly began to return. The churning, acidic sea of my inner life calmed, and I found myself less tormented by my thoughts, less incited to intense emotion by the past as it played in my mind. I could remember but not relive, recount without relaunching into the emotions of those difficult days. I began to see my own faults in the matter, the ways I had only made things worse. And peace came. Not completely and not in every case. But it came and is still coming even now.

I should say, too, that I was motivated in all of this as much by a desire to escape what I had become as by a desire to be right in my attitude toward all of these people. Not only was I convicted by the biblical truths I've shared above, but I also came across this quote from Frederic Buechner's *Wishful Thinking*. It scared me. Listen:

> Of the Seven Deadly Sins, anger is possibly the most fun. To lick your wounds, to smack your lips over grievances long past, to roll over your tongue the prospect of bitter confrontations still to come, to savor to the last toothsome morsel both the pain you are given and the pain you are giving back—in many ways it is a feast fit for a king. The chief drawback is that what you are wolfing down is yourself. The skeleton at the feast is you.[28]

These words set me to thinking about some people I had known in my life who were not likely to end well. They were an angry, snarling breed who were too tied to the pain of their past to make anything meaningful of their lives. They had built monuments to that pain in the hearts of their children as well, and there was a long list of former wives and friends who had long since been driven away. I could envision them in old age, recounting to those who could not escape them the tales of their wounding and their woes. They would die small and scarred and they would never fully understand that they had missed a greater destiny, that they could have walked in a much more lush land than the desert they had made of their lives.

So I forgave. I did it because I was afraid not to. I did it because I hated what I was becoming. I did it because I wanted my God to forgive me and I knew I had made this impossible thus far. I did it because I did not want to be Buechner's skeleton at the feast, and I did it because I wanted to live out a higher plan—not the one the devil had for me that was fashioned in hurt and hatred, but the one chosen for me by a loving God before time even began. And I knew forgiving was the key.

Finally, this: do not go to the next chapter until you have made these truths your own, not just in your mind but in the experience of your soul. This is the crucible of your life's battle and you must not hurry away until the enemy of your soul surrenders all.

CHAPTER 6

Truths for Getting Whole

THERE IS AN EPISODE IN THE LIFE OF JESUS that should have special meaning for us now. It comes to us from the seventeenth chapter of Luke (vv. 11-19) and if we take a moment to peer behind the words we find some truths that will help untie a few of the knots in our souls.

Luke tells us that Jesus was on his way to Jerusalem and that he decided to walk along the border between the regions of Samaria and Galilee. As he started to enter a village, ten lepers called out to him: "Master, have pity on us!"

Jesus did not hesitate. He immediately told them to "go, show yourselves to the priests," for this was as God commanded after a cure (Leviticus 14:1-32). And as the lepers went, they were healed.

The exact word that Jesus used here is important. Luke says that the ten lepers were "cleansed." The Greek word is *katharizo*: it means to "make clean," to remove "physical stains and dirt, as in the case of utensils." In other words, it means to make the surface clean, to remove the dirt that exists on the top.

This was marvelous indeed. We can imagine these lepers walking on the road toward the priests. They must have been uncertain. They wanted to obey Jesus but they also knew that they were not allowed to approach the priests. Or anyone else for that matter. They were lepers and the law required that they live apart from society and, worse, apart from their families. They even had to carry a bell with them everywhere and ring it to warn others that someone unclean was approaching. They probably would have been feeling a jumble of emotions as they went, but then one of them must have noticed that a change had occurred. They were cleansed. The rotting disease that defined their lives was gone. No longer the eroded features. No longer the deformity and the bloody sores. No longer the skin eaten away like a judgment from God. Now they were as other men.

They must have wept. They must have danced and hugged each other and shouted with newfound joy. And then one of them knew what he must do. He turned, leaving the confirmations of the priest to a later time, and he ran back to throw himself at the feet of Jesus. It is important to know that by this time, Jesus had probably arrived inside the village he had been entering when the lepers first called to him. It means that this now-cleansed leper risked stoning to rush into that village, with people who knew him looking on, and all to throw himself at the feet of the one who had delivered him. Jesus must have taken note.

The original language of this passage tells us that this man declared the "splendor of God" as he approached and then flung himself at the feet of his Lord. Jesus was touched and turned the moment into a lesson for the crowd: "Were not all ten cleansed?" he asked. "Where are the other nine? Was no one found to return and give praise to

God except this foreigner?" (vv. 17-18). It was a biting comment and Jesus intended every word. He was standing in a Jewish village and rushing to him in praise was a man who did not care that he might be stoned—both because he was a leper who had not yet been pronounced clean and because he was an unclean Samaritan whom the Jews despised. He simply knew he must give thanks, must declare the splendor of his God. And Jesus made sure the crowd knew that this supposedly doubly unclean man was showing greater faith than all of them.

Turning to the man he said simply, "Rise and go; your faith has made you well" (v. 19). Again, the choice of words is important. Luke captures it faithfully. Jesus had not simply declared what was already true. He did not tell the man he was "cleansed": *katharizo*. No, Jesus was doing something new, something beyond what all ten lepers have known.

Jesus told the man he had been made "well." Our English word is weak in light of the Greek. The word is *sozo*. In this case, it means not just that the man had been cleaned at the surface, but that he was made whole. Or, more exactly, that the man was "saved" from the effects of the disease, and not just the disease itself.

This distinction is important. You see, all the lepers had been cleansed, meaning that the leprosy had been removed from their skin. But there was something deeper that needed healing and only one of the ten received it.

We should know that the day a man was declared a leper was the worst day of his life to that point and that he would know no better days afterward. Once the priest pronounced him unclean, he was immediately forced away from society. He was required to tear his clothes and keep his hair unkempt. The lower part of his face was always to be covered and this meant he would never be seen openly by another human being again. His children were torn from his arms and his wife was free to move on. He was nearly dead, for in the stark words of the law regarding a leper, "He must live alone; he must live outside the camp."

It grew worse. He was not allowed to enter the temple courts just as he was not allowed to enter the camp. We must remember that this was in an age when God revealed himself in specific locations and the leper was banned from each of these locations. So not only was leprosy an isolation from other men, it was also the harshest form of isolation from God.

> **Jesus did not tell the leper he was "cleansed." Jesus told the man he had been made "well."**

We can easily imagine what this must have done to the soul. A man was cursed, left in the wilderness to be eaten alive by a wasting disease. He passed his days alone and must have spent hours wondering what he had done to deserve such a fate. He surely concluded that God had abandoned him. There could be no deeper rejection, no more agonizing loneliness, and no more grinding punishment than to live as a leper—"alone . . . outside the camp." Clearly, the leprosy of the soul—the shriveling, excruciating inner effect of this curse of God—was even worse than the leprosy of the skin.

And, of course, Jesus knew. He knew when he sent the ten away that their skin was not all that needed restoring. So when the one still inwardly leprous Samaritan risked all to give God his due, Jesus finished the work and made the man whole—removing the cruel imprint of the curse upon his soul. Undoing what all the rejection and taunts and loneliness and damning had created inside. For this one, Jesus first cleaned the surface and then cleaned him inside.

This is what we have come to in ourselves as well. If you have given yourself to the truths in the last few chapters, you have become more biblical in your view of people, you have mined some lessons from your season in hell, and you have taken the time to start the process of forgiving. You have done well, and many a lesser soul might have ended the journey here.

But I urge you to consider that your season of bitterness and anger—that period during which you took the bait of offense and found yourself trapped and poisoned of soul—left an imprint that you still need to address. You are like the ten lepers who experienced a cleansing of the surface. You are experiencing much the same. As you forgive, you are allowing God to clean up the mess and start making your life right again. The demonic taunts are coming to an end. Peace is returning. Perhaps relationships are even being restored, and your faith is rising. On the wings of forgiveness your life is being returned to you, and this is no small thing.

Yet there is a deeper work to be done and it is the matter of making you whole and not just outwardly cleansed. To return to the meaning of the Greek words, we want the disease removed, yes, but we also want its effects on our inner lives lifted as well.

Let's take a few moments, then, before we move on, and put ourselves in a position to welcome a deeper work of God. Let us, like that tenth leper, not rush on in the joy of what is new, but let's expand the work so that the restoration brings joy for the rest of our lives.

I think it is best to do this with another list. This will help keep your thoughts organized, allow you to process with friends, and perhaps, when the right time comes, help you bring wholeness to others who are walking where you've been.

There is one truth in Scripture that has been so hotly debated among Christians through the centuries that we often lose the practical impact of it on our lives. It is the idea of predestination—or God determining events in advance. Because this truth is usually debated as a matter of how we become Christians—do we choose God or does he choose us?—it has led to some of the biggest fights in church history. Those holding the idea of free will challenge those who believe in a more divinely fixed fate, with Calvinists debating Arminians and Baptists debating Presbyterians. Frankly, it is not likely to end.

Yet, if I may sidestep that contested territory for a moment, I'd like to talk about the practical importance of God's choosing in advance without necessarily having to solve the gigantic issue of how we get saved. For the moment, I am more concerned with how we view the events of our lives, particularly when it comes to our suffering.

It moves me to hear Paul tell the Thessalonians that they should not be concerned about the trials that Paul and his team were enduring because, "You know quite well that we were destined for them."[29] It is an attitude that we rarely hear from those going through hard times, and yet the words fell freely from Paul's pen and even more readily from his worldview.

Paul took comfort in the idea that the lives of believers unfold as God wills, according to at least a broad plan God designed from before time. Most of us know the Scriptures that form the pillars of this view. We know that God determines "the end from the beginning" so we are not surprised when Jeremiah is told that before he was even conceived God had set a purpose for his life. We are also not surprised when the psalmist writes that God had numbered his days before even one of them was lived.[30] And when Paul says that he wanted to take hold of that for which Christ Jesus had taken hold of him—in other words that there is a purpose for which Jesus had called him—we know that this passion grew from a heartfelt confidence in God's predetermined will.

What we often forget is that this predetermining work of God applies both to the good and to the bad that befalls us. Ephesians 2:10 tell us that God determines wonderful works for us to do and that he determined these works before time began. This is thrilling and makes us eager to storm the future in faith. Yet, the more difficult side of this truth is that our hardships are often predetermined too. This is what Paul was alluding to when he said that he and his band of ministers were "destined" for their trials.

It is a doctrine that should create a wonderfully liberating approach to life. We move forward confidently, knowing that we are living out a plan—at least in the broad sense—that God has determined for our lives. We don't fear hardship because we know that it is part of this plan. We've read that we must go through many hardships to enter the Kingdom of God and we understand that God uses difficulties to shape our lives for his glory. Hard times are painful, but also redemptive—meaning that in the hand of God they accomplish good things in our lives. Knowing this, we can take the attitude of James as expressed in the beautiful Phillips paraphrase of the Bible, and make it our own: "When all kinds of trials and temptations crowd into your lives, my brothers, don't resent them as intruders, but welcome them as friends! Realise that they come to test your faith and to produce in you the quality of endurance. But let the process go on until that endurance is fully developed, and you will find you have become men of mature character."[31]

Now, here comes the hard part. I want you to apply this to your life. I want you to realize a principle that you will naturally want to reject: the hardship of your painful church experience is redemptive in the hand of God and it may even have been ordained.

I know, I know. We want to feel it otherwise. We want to see the hard things that befall us as some strange invader from another world. But they aren't. Not if Scripture is true. Hard things are as much ordained as the blessings and at the very least we can arrive at a state in which we can say with the psalmist, "It was good for me to be afflicted so that I might learn your decrees."[32]

We should have this attitude because it is rooted in the truth of God, but there are also some wonderful benefits that come from having this view. First, when you realize that wounding experiences are often ordained and useful, it draws out some of the poison of your pain. You understand what you have endured as a process in the hand of God rather than a unique and vicious conspiracy against you. This may not lessen the pain but it does change the meaning of the pain, and it may serve as a barrier to the bitterness that wants to taint your soul.

Second, seeing your hurtful season through the lens of God's truth can take your focus off of the people who harmed you. If this hardship was ordained of God and if it is a tool he is using to carve Christ's image in your life, then you can't stay angry at the people who might have wronged you as though they were the sole instigators of it all. Now you can see them as playing their role—yes, perhaps hurtfully to you—but playing out a role nevertheless that wasn't as personally intended as their actions may have seemed. Your focus can now rise from them to the purposes of God. In other words, you can adopt the attitude of Joseph, who was horribly treated by his brothers but once he better understood the work of God in his life was able to say to them, "You intended to harm me, but God intended it for good to accomplish what is now being done, the saving of many lives."[33]

This leads us, then, to the third benefit, which is this: like Joseph, you can get on with the ultimate reason for what you have endured. Notice that Joseph could say to his brothers, "Yes, I realize you were trying to hurt me, but God had a higher purpose and he used your sin for my benefit so that now I can do good to others. I'm not focused on how you wronged me: I'm focused on the good I can now do." This is the ultimate victory, isn't it? The loftiest statement of your cleansing and redemption—after all the pain you've endured—is that now you realize what God was doing and you can get on with that high calling for your life.

Hard things are as much ordained as blessings. At the very least we can say with the psalmist, "It was good for me to be afflicted so that I might learn your decrees."

Now, you have to fight for this. Self-pity will try to take root. Bitterness will offer you its poison. Disillusionment will try to take you out for a meal. Battle all this. Memorize the Scriptures that speak of preordained suffering as well as those that proclaim your destiny to be conformed to the image of Christ. Make Ephesians 2:10 and Romans 8:29 your own. And then stand guard at the portals of your heart and do not let that foreign spirit of resentment settle in.

You are destined for your hardships because you are destined for great works of God. This truth should be your banner, the chant you should cry aloud as you battle through to a liberated heart.

It would be nice if pain was just pain and that was the end of it. You've put up with the betrayal of your friends or that bruising from your church, and how I would love to tell you that when the pain is done, the damage is as well.

Oh, how I wish that were true!

But the truth is, when it comes to emotional pain—the pain that registers inside—the greatest damage is often the thing that continues to resonate when the feeling of the pain subsides. It is that message that the pain tells us about ourselves and about the meaning of our lives.

Some brilliant Christian writers, John Eldredge and Brent Curtis, have described this beautifully in their book, *The Sacred Romance*. I can't recommend their writings enough. Among their many transformational insights, they describe the message that our hurts send to our soul as "the message of the arrows." It is an image that can help you heal and reclaim the higher purpose of your life.

In those good old cowboy movies, someone would shoot an arrow with a written message wrapped around the shaft. In one film I recently saw, a friendly Indian wanted to warn his cowboy friends of imminent danger. So he wrote a note on a small piece of paper, tied it around the arrow, and shot that arrow perfectly into a tree right by the head of his cowboy buddy. Message received. Our cowboy, by the way, read the message and then rolled the paper into a cigarette. Ah, for the days when men were men.

Eldredge and Curtis use this picture of the arrow to describe our wounds. This isn't hard to imagine. When we are insulted or betrayed, when people wound us with their words or their actions, their deeds stick like arrows into our souls. They pierce. They make us bleed. They open an ugly gash until they are removed and then, with time, we heal.

But the damage done to us is not just the wound but the meaning of the wound. You see, every arrow that hits its mark in our souls has a message attached. It is a message that makes a statement about our lives, about why the arrow was sent to do damage in the first place. And it is this message that lives longer than the pain of the arrow, enters our inner beings, and starts spreading its damning message into our hearts. It is this message of the arrows that often does the more lasting harm.

Let us say that some friends band together to exclude you from their plans. They are going to cut you off and make sure you don't know about something they all intend to do together. They all come from wealthy families and they know you can't afford what they are about to do. They've talked about this and made their jokes. They've worked themselves into such an attitude of superiority that even though they have planned something fun, they've conspired to keep you away. And you find out and you are hurt that they've intentionally not included you in their plans. This is the arrow. But it is the message of the arrow that is actually the more damaging blow. You come from an inferior family, a lesser tribe, a poorer breed. So much so that you know your friends are embarrassed to be with you. So the message of their actions takes root in your soul and, if you don't know how to defend yourself, you make this message your own: "I am somehow inferior. I guess I'll always be poor. No wonder my friends are embarrassed to be with me." This message summons other messages like it from other arrows fired into your life. Soon you have made a case to yourself that you are a social leper because of your financial status; no wonder others refuse to draw near. Now, a one-time event from which you were excluded becomes a lifetime certainty of your soul.

This is the power of the message of the arrows and I discovered my own version of this in the church hurt I endured. Remember that the church I pastored had a huge staff and many of these leaders were my friends. As Christian friends ought to do, we regularly shared our challenges and our failings when we gathered to strengthen each other and to pray. So I would share my heart openly and let them see the warping of my soul and the areas of my life where Christ-likeness had yet to reign. I shared, for example, that I didn't have the best relationship with my father and that it was difficult for me to forgive those who wronged me. I even shared good things about my life, such as that my mother miscarried a number of children until I was finally born and that I was particularly dear to my parents as a result.

Now, all of this received a knowing nod and a compassionate prayer from my fellow leaders at the time. Yet later, when relationships soured and the goal became to wound as deeply as possible, the things I had shared in transparent moments were reworked through psychobabble into a basis for doing me harm. I was, one elder proclaimed, a man with "father issues" who was given to rejection and fear. This had made me hard-hearted, stubborn, and unable to forgive. Even the sweet story of my birth became a basis for insult. Clearly, my mother's fear at the possibility of losing me had reached me in the womb and given me rejection issues and a "codependency" that had ruled me all my life.

So by sharing my life with friends during tender times of prayer, I simply provided information that could later be used to show just how debilitated I was by my wounds and how tainted I was by my past. And soon the message took flight: "You are damaged, Stephen Mansfield—too rejected and fear-ridden to be of any use. Bitterness has poisoned your soul and anger drives you to destruction. We cannot love you, will not even treat you with the honor your years of service deserve. Be gone and roam the wilderness as your punishment. We cannot even be kind to you, so horrible is the state of your life."

Even when the day came that I plucked out the arrows, the message tied to each shaft had already seeped into my heart. And this message reorganized my memories of my life, and before long everything I had experienced seemed to offer evidence of what they had said. So the curse was upon me and, for a while, I roamed the wilderness in disgust at myself, sure that every word on the message of the arrows was true.

Thankfully, we heal. We push the splinter to the surface as the soul strives to reclaim what it means to be whole. And we realize that truth is often a matter of degree. Yes, I would like to have had a better relationship with my father and yes I have felt rejected or angry or afraid in my life. This sounds to me like what it means to be human. But no, I'm not some unique kind of monster who doesn't deserve kindness and grace. So I reject the message of the arrows, and I allow my memories to re-form according to truth. My life is not cursed and I will not bear scars because a small group of men used my holy attempts at transparency to justify themselves.

Jesus, help me find truth. Jesus, help me forgive. Jesus, let your truth erase the message of the arrows shot angrily into my soul.

Now, my recovering friend, you must do the same. Perhaps you have forgiven and hopefully you have prayed to be cleansed. You are recovering yourself and, more importantly, you are being recovered and restored by God. But you must also look carefully at what you have come to believe as a result of your wounds. You must ask yourself about the message of the arrows in your life. Otherwise, you can forgive and even believe that your wounding was ordained, but you will still believe things about yourself that will keep you from wholeness and make you fall short of the destined purpose for your life. They will also lead to agony and torment of soul. Look at the messages of the arrows, decide what is true, and do the work you already know how to do in order to stand against the lies and the undue shame.

I ended the last section with the word *shame* on purpose. I want to ponder its meaning with you and apply it to your life. Let me tell you my point clearly from the very beginning: people who are deeply hurt often live afterward with a deep sense of shame. This is true, yet to fully understand it we have to know a bit more about the meaning of shame.

We tend to think of the word *shame* in terms of guilt or embarrassment over something that we've done wrong. We got caught with our hand in the cookie jar or telling a big juicy lie. We went bankrupt and all our friends knew about it and, oh, what shame hovered over our lives.

While some of the biblical words for shame certainly can be interpreted this way, there is another English word that could be used for shame. For example, when the psalmist says, "Lord, do not let me be ashamed," he is actually using the word *doomed*.

I like using this word because it is more modern and comes closer to describing the impact that shame can have in our lives. To feel doomed means to believe that cycles of hurt and embarrassment govern your life. It means to be cursed, to be condemned to bad things happening. And this sense of impending negativity often embeds itself in us during horrible seasons of wounding and insult. Somehow we walk away believing that we deserved our mistreatment and that therefore we are likely to endure it again. In other words, what happened to us is a product of something within us that makes us a magnet for harm. We are doomed, cursed with unending cycles of pain.

The corollary of this kind of thinking is what we believe about those who are free from doom. Come on, you know them. They are the beautiful people.

These people wake up every morning in their beautiful homes, shake their beautiful heads of hair, kiss their astonishingly beautiful spouses, and strike out into their beautiful lives. Their children are, you guessed it, beautiful. At breakfast there is always enough milk and if the toast falls to the floor it lands with the jellied side up—not like it does for those who are doomed. We are talking about the beautiful people here, after all.

The beautiful people shine out at the world with their beautiful teeth and they slip so gracefully through the raindrops that they barely get wet. Their work always prospers and their kids always rise and they will always be happy because they are the opposite of doomed. They are blessed with continuous cycles of happiness and good fortune.

This, of course, is all a flaming lie. But it is what we tell ourselves when we feel doomed. Our sense of doom, more often than not, comes from a deep experience of hurt in which we determined that something about us made this happen. This is not the message of the arrows. This is what you said to yourself in an attempt to give some meaning to the hurt you experienced. "This didn't just happen," you said in your mind. "I must be a magnet for treatment of this kind. I must in some invisible way order the cosmos to cause myself and others pain. I can see it in the eyes of my children and in the disgust of the people in my life. I am doomed and this cycle of pain is never going to end."

I want to tell you something I have seen. There are people who have been deeply hurt. But they rose up, forgave, saw their hurts as tools in the hand of God, and even rejected the false messages that those hurts tried to send. But yet, their hurt was so deep and the agonies they endured so deforming that they never shook their sense of doom. And though they were successful and though most of their friends looking on from the outside would never have known, these people secretly nursed the most debilitating fear that it would all happen again, that somehow their lot in the world was to cycle through unending punishment and pain.

You know this isn't true. It is a lie that the shock to your soul left you believing. And you have to destroy it. Now. You have to take a long look at yourself and see if the haunting of doom is already ruining your life. Do you see the world as divided between people like you, the Tribe of the Doomed, and, on the other side, the beautiful people? Do you expect, despite your success and your blessings that another punishing season is sure to arrive? Do you fear for your spouse and your children because you know they are attached to this bruising dynamic of your life? Do you lay awake at night wondering when a new session of hell will announce itself?

If so, doom is at work in your life. You believe you are cursed, bound to dark turnings of fate. And your life is being damaged by a lie.

Don't rush by this. Don't hurry to turn the page. This one requires some quiet and some time to explore your own mind. And you probably have to do this one alone. You might be tempted to ask someone else to help, but those who feel doomed usually hide their fears from everyone close.

You are not cursed.
You were just hurt.
Don't let a lie
keep you from
what you were
made to be.

Lord, help us expose the imprint of doom in our souls.

And once you have found it, you know what to do. Hold it before God as the lie that it is. Wash it out of your soul with the truths of God's Word. Expose it to others so the light of truth and the help of comrades can drive the darkness away. And seed the opposite of doom—a destined life of blessing, of wholeness, and of meaningful service to God—into the lives in your family. Quietly go to war for the generations to come. You are not cursed. You were just hurt. Don't let a lie keep you from what you were made to be.

I have a friend, a college basketball coach, who is always threatening to write a book called "Demons I Have Known and Loved." It is a joke, really. You see, he is wonderfully gifted in helping people get free from the bondages that ruin their lives. In fact, he was one of those pastors I mentioned who intervened in my situation and helped to rescue me from the mess. But the truth is he is never going to write this book he keeps talking about. So, I'm going to steal his idea and use his truths here. I'm only doing this to help you and for the glory of God, you understand. But I am stealing, nevertheless. Here goes.

People get nervous when we talk about demons and I think with good reason. You see, most of what people think they know about Satan and his kingdom does not come from the Bible but rather from horror movies and Stephen King novels. This should be no surprise. Half a dozen surveys have shown that Christians spend far more time watching television and movies than they do reading their Bibles. So it is no wonder that we have confused the biblical view of the demonic with the gospel according to *The Exorcist*. This is why we fear that demons make people's heads spin around or make them crawl around on the ceiling.

The problem is not only our bad theology but it is also that we think the only time demons are at work is when something dramatic is happening. In other words, if we hear that someone passed out and began reciting the Lord's Prayer backward in Latin, then we are fairly sure the devil is involved. But if something more mundane takes place, like a drug addiction or a crumbling marriage or a teenager being enticed into a cult, our theology of the demonic usually isn't broad enough to shed any light.

Let me tell you something that will come as a surprise. There is no Greek word in the New Testament that means "demon possessed." I know this sounds odd since we read the words *demon possessed* throughout the English version of the New Testament. Also, our years of watching horror movies make us focus on the possession side of what demons do more than anything else. But the truth is that the word in New Testament Greek that we translate as "demon possession" also means a great deal more. The word is *daimonizomai* and it is probably best translated "demonized." If we used it the right way, it would apply to a whole range of demonic activity against human beings—from possessing people to blowing up your toaster and hiding your keys.

I don't mean to be trite. But because we learn more from movies than the Bible, we tend to think that demons possess people and that's it. They have no other job description. Instead, the Bible describes a whole range of activity that demons get involved in, from possessing to gaining a foothold in a person's life, and from suggesting false doctrines to blinding people's minds so they can't understand truth. The Bible gives us a long list describing what the devil and his demons are capable of doing, and most of it is captured in this all-inclusive word that should be translated "demonized."

There is another truth you should know before we make application of these facts to your life. One of the things demons do is reinforce immorality in the lives of people who give themselves over to moral uncleanness. Now let's be careful here. Am I saying that someone who is immoral is demon possessed? (I suppose we should probably stop using that term for our purposes here.) But the answer to that question is no. We all engage in immorality and usually it is an act of our will that more than likely has no connection to demons at all. However, having said this, the truth is that once someone gives himself or herself to immorality, a demonic force may well take the occasion of that sin and move in to reinforce the moral uncleanness, to build a stronghold, and to try to gain control.

This is why demons in the Bible are often named according to what they do. Yes, we are told about the names of some spirits, like Legion or Apollyon and such. But usually the Bible speaks of demons by their function. For example, we are told of lying spirits, spirits of prostitution, spirits of fear, spirits of impurity, and even spirits of divination.

Let's say for example that a man has a problem with lying. He knows it is wrong but he cannot seem to keep himself from telling lies. He repents often and sometimes he even apologizes to those he has lied to. But in time, he gets used to this lifestyle of lying. His conscience gets hardened and he is less sensitive to the wrong of what he is doing. Now up until this point, he has made his own decisions. He has not been dominated by any spiritual force, nor is he even close to what we have called demon possession. Yet because the devil and his demons come to kill, steal, and destroy, and because they want to dominate the man in our example and keep him from his destiny, a demon starts to move in. He is going to try to strengthen the hold that lying has on this man's life. He is going to suggest lies and deepen this man's gift for deception and generally do everything in his power to make lying a controlling motivator in this man's life. Is this man possessed? No, but there is a stronghold in his life nonetheless and that stronghold is demonically reinforced. In other words, he is "demonized" in the way we should use this word, though he is not "demon possessed" in the old sense of the phrase.

My friend the basketball coach knows this truth about how demons work. He understands that good Christians who want to please God can nevertheless give themselves so intently to an area of uncleanness that demons soon get involved. He also knows that Christians fail to recognize this work of demons because they think demons are only at work if something more dramatic and horror-movie-like is happening.

But my coach friend also knows something else and it is the reason he wanted to call his book Demons I Have Known and Loved. That is, before I stole his idea! From his long experience in ministry, Coach knows that what keeps some people from dealing with demonic influence is the fact that they like the part of themselves where the demons are working. In other words, a demon or demons have set up a stronghold in a part of their personality that they don't want to change, an area that they like about who they are or how they live. So in truth, they are voluntarily partnering with demons.

This sounds extreme, but it is actually just normal Christian truth. Let's say that a man—let's call him Sean—comes from a long line of ancestors with explosive tempers. In fact, let's say that Sean is Irish and he actually is proud that his people have big, bold tempers. It is part of his heritage. He appreciates this aspect of himself. He is usually fairly loving, as the Irish tend to be, but when he is pushed past a certain point he can explode into a fuming rage. And he kind of likes it. He enjoys the force that inflames his soul and the way that language roars from him—sometimes it's almost Shakespearean. And he relishes the power that his temper gives him over people. He sees them acting afraid and scurrying to do what he says and it makes him feel strong and brave.

Now if Sean is a Christian, we can be sure that a demonic force might move in on such an unclean dynamic in his life and try to make his anger an even more controlling stronghold. We can surmise that this demonic force might even try to push Sean to other, accompanying strongholds. For example, if Sean is willing to give himself to rage, then why not violence or vengeance or drink? Why not swearing or stealing or strife? All of these can be related in some way to anger.

So you already see the problem. If a pastor comes to Sean and says, "My brother, I sense a real stronghold of anger in your life and I think there is a demonic presence behind it. Why don't you let me help you get free?"—well, you can imagine that this might not be good news to Sean. He likes being his version of Irish, how it makes him feel and what it allows him to do. So he really wants to protect this part of himself and may not be open to God's best, which is becoming a peaceful, spirit-controlled man. No, Sean is clinging to demons he has known and loved. He knows the spirit of rage and he likes him. In fact, he welcomes him to dinner and offers him food. The two have become good friends. And that is why Sean may never be free.

Now, you probably already know what I want to ask you: are there demons in your life that you have known and loved? You see, if I had asked this question without explaining all that I have, you might have responded, "No, there are no demons in my life! What do you mean? I'm not possessed! I don't spew green vomit or throw priests out the window. What are you talking about?" But now you know that I'm not talking about anything so dramatic—though I am talking about something just as serious.

Are your church hurts and that season of humiliation and pain in any way involved with a stronghold in your life? Is there an aspect of your personality that you tend to like but which is actually sin and which exacerbated the problems you have endured? Are there demons you have known and loved?

I'm not asking these questions to torment you, but to keep you from living out your damage again and again. Most of us have probably seen the movie *Groundhog Day*. The actor Bill Murray plays a character who has to live the same day over and over again until he lives it right. And, when he finally does, he gets to move on in life. A new day finally dawns, even though previously he had been trapped in the same old day again and again.

Is there an aspect of your personality that you tend to like but which is actually sin? Are there demons you have known and loved?

I want you to be whole so you can live out your new days. But I've been helping people through their hurts enough to know that some folks are living their own hellish version of *Groundhog Day*, all because they are clinging to the very forces that are going to keep them bound to the old patterns and locked out of the new.

What is the truth about you? Combine all that you've learned in this book—about how to hear truth from the mouths of your critics, about how to identify your idols, and about how to walk free of the strongholds you've helped to make in your life—and see if you can't hold this truth of demons you have known and loved up to your life. Is your bondage anger? Is it lying? Is it a tendency to rebel against authority or control people with vain little conspiracies and power plays? What is it? Be ruthless and find out what is dominating your life. Ask your friends, but only if they are godly friends and brave enough to tell you the truth to your face. Your spouse or a good friend can surely help as well, if you will humble yourself and be quiet for a while. But don't cut this process short. This may be the most important issue of all in your life and you have to search intently as the Holy Spirit gives you light.

Once you have found your areas of bondage and partnership with spirits of evil, start repenting of that area of sin. This removes the "landing zone" for the devil and starts to loosen his grip. Then, once you've thoroughly repented and you are sure your sins are cleansed by Jesus' blood, gather a group of fellow believers to pray that you can drive that evil off. Find people who are experienced at this and, if they are solidly biblical and not overly weird, ask them for help. And then start making a change. Walk in the opposite spirit from whatever has controlled you, and feed yourself on examples and Scriptures that help you find a different script for your life, a different programming for your soul. And if you find that your case is severe, see a good, Spirit-empowered counselor and let him or her help you make the changes you need. You cannot do this alone, and this may be the first time in a while you have had to admit that you need the body of Christ, and that Christianity is a team sport and not an individual event.

However you go about it, you are truly free of your church hurt and its negative fruit in your life only if you send away the demons you have known and loved. And hear me on this, you absolutely must do it. Your calling demands it. Any hope of peace for the rest of your days demands it. Walking free of even more church hurts in the future demands it. And that spouse whom you love and those kids in the next room deserve it: a spiritual heritage that is holy and clean.

So, then, these are the four truths I want you to explore, to apply to your life, and to use to truly be whole.

+ View your sufferings as something ordained by and useful in the hand of God.
+ Defeat the message of the arrows.
+ Dispel the curse of doom that may have gathered in your life.
+ Drive off any of the demons you may have known and loved.

These all are essential—even after you have forgiven and examined your hellish season for the wisdom it might grant you. These courses of action based on truths can be pillars of wholeness in your life.

And before we move on, I want you to know why this matter of being whole and not just cleansed is so important. As we've discussed in earlier pages, you have a destiny and a calling to fulfill. You have years that stretch out before you like a huge canvas under the paintbrush of God, a masterpiece waiting to be revealed. And I desperately want you to come to the end of your life and be able to say of yourself what was said of David in Acts 13:36: he fulfilled God's will in his generation and was buried with his fathers.

Yet, I have seen too much to believe that this happens automatically.

I have worked with some of the most powerful, talented people of our age and yet I have watched them descend into disaster under the press of the deformities of their soul. I have worked with rock stars whose gifts were admired worldwide, yet watched as they have crashed while many of us stood knowingly by, not surprised that a combination of pride and untended wounding led to their day of humiliation. I have also watched men who influenced thousands, perhaps millions, for Jesus and who then let the knotted condition of their inner lives lead them to destruction and thus taint everything they had done.

So, you understand why I'm not satisfied with anything less than wholeness for your life. It is not enough that the mess is cleaned up, like a house being prepared for company. We can only be satisfied when the condition of our hearts that led to the mess in the first place is challenged, healed, and turned onto a healthy, Christlike path.

This is what happens when God fully redeems, and it is what is essential if you hope to live out your days as that masterpiece God has ordained. We don't want you to rise quickly from your pains and then crash again. We want a long, steady ascent to the heights of your calling, with no embarrassing moral explosions once you reach the heights of your destiny. God has a way chosen for you and only your refusal to allow a pure and complete work in your life can keep this chosen way from unfolding.

Go hard at it then. The price is worth paying to hear Jesus say "Well done."

CHAPTER 7

Coming Home

THE TWO MEN WALKED THEIR SEVEN-MILE JOURNEY from Jerusalem to Emmaus, kicking stones in disgust as they went. They stood out a bit from the other travelers on the road that day, for their pace was slow and their faces betrayed the shattering disappointment in their hearts.

A man approached whom they did not know and he asked about the heaviness in their manner and the tortured rhythm of their words. Their faces did not change as they spoke and they came close to rebuking this stranger in their reply. "Are you the only one who doesn't know what has happened? There was a man named Jesus of Nazareth who was a prophet. He was awesome and did powerful things in front of huge crowds. But the authorities arrested him and then had him killed. I guess the bottom line is that we had hoped he was the One, but he's been dead for three days and it doesn't seem like he is going to rise from the dead as he said he would. And adding to everything, several women think they met an angel who said this Jesus was alive.

Everyone is in a stir and no one knows what to believe and we were so disgusted we just decided to leave the city. But it's all so tragic, because, like I said, we had hoped he was the One."[34]

You know the rest. It is Jesus who stands before them and he chides them for their doubt and gives them a Bible lesson that we wish we could have heard. Then, when the three pull aside and dine together, Jesus gives them what we now know is Communion—the Eucharist, the Supper of the Lord—and the Bible tells us that then, but only then, did they recognize him before Jesus quickly disappeared. And they were left there in wonder, marveling at how their hearts burned within them as he spoke and at how they knew him in the breaking of the bread.

It is a moving story—of the tenderness of Jesus and how the truth can set men free; of the power of the holy, broken bread; and of the certainty of Scripture to explain the death of Christ. And yet, for our purposes in these pages, there is also a sour phrase in this story, one that echoes in our own experience. It is almost a plea, an expression that people have repeated through the centuries as they wrestled with God and the hard things they had to endure.

"We had hoped . . ."

It is all there, isn't it? Can't you feel it? Hope. That surging strength of expectation, the thrill of what we believe is promising to occur. The bond with those who share our vision and who dare to own it with us in their hearts. And then: *We had hoped.* The report of the disappointed, the confession of all those who have dared to believe. *We had hoped.* It is what we say on the other side, when our vision is shattered and we feel ourselves to be fools for trusting in something we couldn't even see.

You and I have said this, after our church hurt, when we no longer belonged and we looked back on all we had hoped for. We may feel silly and clumsy now and maybe we can't believe how far we are from all that filled those days. But we were devoted and we wanted to play a role. And then the turmoil rolled in like an Atlantic storm and now we find ourselves all these hours of pain away.

I suspect that we can utter those desperate words along with the two men on the road to Emmaus. *We had hoped.* Yes, admit it with me. As cool as I've tried to be, after all the embarrassment and questioning and fights, I have to acknowledge that I lived for too long in the shadow of those three words.

I had hoped—for friendship and loyalty and for someone to act biblically. I had hoped—for belonging and for truth and for a role to call my own. And most of all, I had hoped for Jesus. For his presence and his comfort and his tender, restoring hand.

And then Jesus came. No, not bodily, in some rapture just for Stephen Mansfield, but in the form of those bruising pastors who busted into my life. He came in that family I lived with for a year. He came in those who took me out for a burger and spoke a rebuilding, encouraging word. And, yes, he came in the words of Patton and Robin Williams and Mel Gibson's *Braveheart* and even *Hellraiser*, believe it or not. But finally, he came as I kneeled at his table, as his bread was broken for me, and my eyes, too, were opened and my heart, too, burned at his words.

And I came home. And I want you to come home, as well.

Your story is likely different from mine. Perhaps the day you walked out of that church is the last time you've ever been back—there or anywhere else. Or maybe you've found a comfortable, protected place at the back of a big cathedral, where no one knows and no one can press in on your scars. Or perhaps you tried to jump right back in and find another church as soon as you could. But in your wounded and bleeding state, it all seemed thin and fearful and not worth the cost. And so you've floated or you've fed where you could on television programs or through books. Or maybe you've simply remade your beliefs so you don't need the people of God anymore.

But now, perhaps, things are different. If you've been tracking with me in this book, you've taken some huge steps and your soul is not now as it was before. Think about it:

+ We've drunk from the lives of great men of history who have endured pain much like our own.
+ We've pondered the human condition and realized that all men are damaged, and this helps us look at our own church hurt in a different light.
+ We dove at length into forgiveness, escaping the traps of bitterness and the damage done to our lives.
+ We surveyed our experience and found out what we could about who we are and about what our souls reached for in our season of crisis.
+ We learned a bit about how to be whole and we did some interior work that is essential for true life in the days ahead.

In a sense, we have had our own Emmaus Road experience: hearing Jesus' words, inviting him in, welcoming his power to change us, and then seeing him as we have not before, at least in a while.

So we should be different now, and when we say "We had hoped," it does not have to be with the longing of those who speak of a country they will never see. It can be with the spirit of a people coming home again, of a people who know they have been gone too long, who have turned their backs on where they belong, and who are now slowly, cautiously, willing to take up those hopes again.

Now let me make something very clear. I am not trying to push you back to where you were. In fact, the last thing I want at this point is for you to go back to church with the same attitudes and expectations that you had before. And I certainly don't care whether you go back to the same church. That is completely up to you.

No, instead I want you to add to your newfound healing of soul a newfound theology of what church—for you, anyway—ought to be. This is where I want to take you now. If you have learned a few things, forgiven, taken stock of yourself, and committed yourself to new wholeness as these pages prescribe, it is time for you to think about reconnecting with the people of God. But first, I want to frame your understanding of what this means in a new and hopefully more biblical way than you have likely known.

Our own Emmaus Road experience is hearing Jesus' words, inviting him in, welcoming his power to change us, and then seeing him as we have not before.

Odd. I'm hearing some music as I write these words. Hmm. It seems to be the Dixie Chicks. I think I can just make out the words. It's from their big old, bitter song, "Not Ready to Make Nice."

I'm not ready to make nice
I'm not ready to back down . . .

Well, obviously we need to turn that music off. In fact, delete that song from your iPod and stop watching the video on YouTube. That isn't your theme song anymore. We'll find one for you, though, maybe even by the time you finish this book.

I want you to risk believing that you will have to approach connecting to a church a bit more formally than you have before. Now I can just hear you saying, "Formally! Oh yeah! I'm not going back to a church unless I have a team of lawyers and a bodyguard at my side!" No, that's not what I mean. I think we need to be a bit less sentimental, a bit less focused on style and pleasure, and a bit more attentive to the pillars of what it means for you to be part of a church. So, now, as you ponder the idea of a new church, keep these signposts in mind.

When we think of joining a church, we usually think of becoming part of a body of people. This isn't too surprising, because the people are the most visible part of the church. Besides, physically speaking, to join them means to plop down right beside them every Sunday. We certainly can't move too far away from this reality, but I want to suggest that as you rebuild your understanding of what it means to belong to a church, focusing on belonging to the people just isn't enough.

In fact, we have a bit of a historic disconnect in what it even means to "join" a church. You see, throughout most of church history—

particularly since the Reformation—a church was produced by a covenant. Christians had noticed that God dealt with humans down through the centuries in a series of covenants, and that even a relationship as tender and romantic as marriage, for example, is described in the Bible as a covenantal relationship. So people began to deal with each other in covenants and this gave the world some wonderful institutions. A federal government, for example, is probably best understood as a covenanted form of government. Even the word *federal* comes from the Latin word, *fedora*, which means—you guessed it— "covenanted." And, of course, business contracts are covenants, and legal oaths of the kind that bind you to the military or confirm a person for political office are a form of covenant also.

This same covenant theology defined churches as well. Usually a church came into being as a result of a formal document that "covenanted" all the people of that group together for certain purposes and under certain authorities. In fact, when people from an earlier time in history spoke of being members of a certain church, what they meant was that they were members of the covenant of that church. Historians can even show us the statements of people who wrote in their letters, for example, "I am a member of the covenant at the Boston church." For them the church certainly wasn't the building and it wasn't even the people; it was the covenant that bound this local expression of the body of Christ to God, to a purpose, and to a prescribed way of relating to each other. In fact, in some of the historic churches in the world, you can even find their founding church covenant framed and hanging on the wall.

Now, this book is not about trying to change the way churches are formed worldwide. If a pastor who is reading this book wants to lead his church toward an older, more covenant theology model, fine with me. But my point here is to urge a different way of approaching church in your mind or in the mind of someone who wants to be a part of a functioning expression of the body of Christ.

I believe that thinking of a church in terms of covenant, even if the church you want to join doesn't have a covenant, has a wonderful way of aligning your vision to what is important before you join. For example, if you are thinking about joining First Church, using the covenantal ideal, you would ask yourself what these people have bound themselves to before God. This would presuppose what their view of God is and lead to what they have bound themselves to in his service. Then, a covenant model—again, even if this model is only in your mind and not in First Church's history—would make you ask how this church is governed, what the people are obligated to do, and hopefully, what impact they intend to have on the world.

It is important for you to realize what a novel approach this is. You see, in our Western culture, choosing a church is like choosing among the seventy-five different kinds of mustard they sell at the store. If you don't like one, you can discard it and pick up another. Because there are so many, you can make a change for any reason at all. Perhaps you don't like the color of the label on this one or the shape of the bottle on these others. No problem. There are sixty-five others to try.

The same is true with churches. In my hometown of Nashville, there are nearly a thousand churches for barely a million people, which means that church hopping is the sport of choice among believers. And the reasons people choose churches can become rather mundane. They like the teaching style of a pastor or this church has a great facility for the kids. The men's group does an annual hunting retreat or there are those great racquetball courts at the Family Life Center. Now don't misunderstand, all of this can be an attraction, but I must tell you that in many of the situations I've helped clean up, people eventually had horrible problems at churches they chose to attend for some unwise reasons. The church they chose wasn't a good fit for them or their family and the pastor was known to be a mess, but it had that beautiful architecture or it was in the upscale area of town or it had that great Sunday school program.

And the walls came tumbling down. Why? Because they didn't ask covenantal questions: How do they view God? What do they think he has called them to do? Who is in charge and what authority do they have? What have they set themselves to do in the world? What do they expect of their members? And are you and your family called in the same way, to the same purposes that these people sense for themselves?

Now, we have moved a bit beyond talking about your former church mess, but it might help you to take a moment to consider this covenant theology and what it says for how you joined that church where you had such troubles. Did you join for lightweight reasons like style or facilities or esteem? Or did you think about their view of God, their doctrine, their governing structure, or what they were committed to do in the world? I have found in my years of helping people deal with their church wounds and helping churches draw the kind of people that fit their vision that this statement is true: almost every time there is a disaster between a member and church, that member gave little thought to the important matters when he or she joined. Hold this thought up against your own church experience and see if this isn't the case. Then, you might want to write down what you got right and what you missed so that you have a guide for your church choice in the future.

Obviously, this covenant approach is helpful, but there are a few other factors I want you to consider. One of them is the question of authority, but hold up—I may not mean what you think.

You have probably realized by now that I think we make bad church choices—and by "bad" I only mean that the church is not a good fit for us—because we get sentimental and make decisions on the wrong basis. You can certainly attend a church because you like the music or because Grandma went there or because it meets in a cute stone building with ivy crawling up the walls, but none of these factors touch the heart of what makes for a good church fit. And on no matter are people more sentimental and misguided than on the matter of the pastor and his or her personal style.

Surveys tend to show that one of the major factors people consider when choosing a church is the style of the lead pastor. Certainly, it is understandable that this should be a factor in their thinking and I hear it all the time:

> *"I like him because he is so funny!"*
> *"He is so loving, and his wife is a real sweetheart."*
> *"He is a stalwart about Scripture, and he is tough on us.*
>   *That's good!"*
> *"He is an older man, and I like that he has some years on him."*

All of these attributes make for a successful pastor, but they alone aren't enough for making a good decision about joining a church. Let's consider for a moment the primary purpose you have a pastor in the first place. In Ephesians 4:11-12, Paul tells us that God gave us pastors for the same reason he gave us apostles, evangelists, prophets, and teachers—"to prepare God's people for works of service, so that the body of Christ may be built up." Now, I want you to keep this truth foremost in your mind: God gives you a pastor to train you for works of service and for using your gifts to the glory of God. This is the heart of the matter and we should not allow ourselves to be distracted from it.

Let's lay this truth alongside something else that Paul describes in 2 Corinthians 10:8. In this passage, Paul is in the process of defending his ministry against critics, and he says, "For even if I boast somewhat freely about the authority the Lord gave us for building you up rather than pulling you down, I will not be ashamed of it." We should focus on the fact that Paul says three things. First, he had authority. Second, it was an authority that extended to the Corinthians. And, third, it was an authority for building them up rather than tearing them down. By the way, Paul says the same thing again a few chapters later. In 2 Corinthians 13:10, he writes, "I write these things when I am absent, that when I come I may not have to be harsh in my use of authority—the authority the Lord gave me for building you up, not for tearing you down."

These verses are an antidote to some of the problems that have plagued our churches of late. There has been a great deal of emphasis in our preaching and theology on submission to pastors and on "covering" and on matters that deal with leaders exercising control over their people. This has even reached a fever pitch in troubled movements like the discipleship or shepherding movements. But Paul gives us a good basis for understanding what a spiritual leader ought to be in our lives, and if we can strip away the sentiment for a moment and be functional about the matter, it will help us live out the wisdom God intends.

If we put together what we've read on this matter from Paul in Ephesians and 2 Corinthians, we find that a good pastor is considered to be a gift from God. He should primarily be about the task of teaching and training us to do works of service to the glory of God. And that pastor should have authority for our lives, but it should be an authority that builds us up and does not tear us down. In other words, the right pastor for us has a brand of authority that reaches into our lives and helps us grow into Christ and into the fruitful, gifted creatures we are destined to be.

If we hold to this definition of pastoring, what is not important becomes immediately clear. Certainly, I would rather listen to a humorous speaker than I would a somber one, but this has nothing to do with equipping me for service or having authority for my life. I suppose, also, that if I were choosing a pastor off a rack, I would prefer an older one, and, yes, one with a sweet wife and one who is fierce in the pulpit. I might also prefer that he played racquetball, liked reading Shakespeare, and loved to eat Chinese food on weekends—because I do all these things. But, again, none of this has anything to do with making me a better man in Christ. In fact, as I look back on my life, some of the most effective pastors I have had were not that articulate, were not that good-looking, and certainly did not possess the kind of pizzazz that would draw a huge crowd.

Yet they had authority for training me and making me what I am called to be.

So now, along with the factors of a covenantal approach to belonging to a church—an approach that considers God, doctrine, structure, and purpose in the world—I want you to think about your future church in terms of whether that pastor or pastoral team carries the authority to build you into your calling. Don't make your choice based on the Wow Factor or the Entertainment Factor or matters of personal charm and style. Choose instead after having listened and experienced for a while, based on whether or not the leadership team of this church will be able to coach you to your destiny and toward your place in the body of Christ.

The right pastor for us has a brand of authority that reaches into our lives and helps us grow into Christ and into the fruitful, gifted creatures we are destined to be.

Again, this might be a good time for you to look back over the church choices you have made in the past, both the successful ones and the ones that did not go well, and learn what you can from the experience. When it all fell apart, was there anything about the way you viewed the pastor or his team that failed you in the end? Did you have any expectations that were unbiblical and unfair to the people in charge? Do you see a pattern in your hopes and demands that you need to repair? Can you find in your experience a time when a pastor truly had authority for equipping you and coaching you in Christ?

Make lists. Write down the good and the bad. Discuss them with your spouse or with those who knew you at the time. It isn't a crime to have chosen badly or to have had expectations that no one could fulfill. But it is folly to ignore the clear counsel of Scripture and start looking for a church in that same unproductive, unbiblical way again.

Now I want you to consider yet a third factor in your decision about a church, but it is rooted in a principle that really should govern all of your life. In fact, this principle, this maxim or truth, is one of the most defining in my life. Here it is: *You have a destiny, but your destiny is fulfilled by investing in the destinies of others.* Let me say it again. Read it slowly.

You have a destiny, but your destiny is fulfilled by investing in the destinies of others.

The first part of this sentence is easy to recognize as true. The Bible teaches repeatedly that we each have a destiny—a specific calling and/or purpose—that is determined in advance by God. For example, from Jeremiah 1:5 we learn that God has set a purpose for us before we were even conceived. Then, in Psalm 139:15-16 we read that we were formed in the womb based on that preset purpose of God. And in Philippians 3:12, we hear Paul declare the passion of a destined life: "I press on to take hold of that for which Christ Jesus took hold of me." All of these Scriptures, and a great many more we could list, confirm that God has predetermined a purpose for our lives. So it is true: you have a destiny.

Yet what we often forget is that our destiny is not fulfilled by focusing on that single destiny and exalting it above all else. No, our destiny is only fulfilled as we invest in the destinies of others. The very gifts God has given us, the very calling on our lives, is about investing our gifts into the lives of others in order to lift *them* to their purpose. This is the pattern Jesus set for us. How did he fulfill his purpose in God? He surrendered his rights, served, invested in others, and laid down his life. This is how we fulfill our purpose, too. And this is why Jesus told us that true greatness is being the servant of all, that we don't really gain our lives until we lose them.

We can tell this is true from the very idea of spiritual gifts. God has called some of us to be pastors and some to be administrators and some to be teachers and some to be given to mercy—among many other gifts. None of these can be done in a room alone. The whole assumption of spiritual gifts is that God gives you an ability to do good in the lives of others.

If you are a pastor, you dig into the lives of others and build them up in Christ. If you are an evangelist, you lead people to Christ and train others to do the same. If you are a prophet, you speak words of power into the lives of others for their good. None of these gifts are for the one gifted. They are for the body of Christ, and yet this is how the gifted one fulfills his calling in Jesus.

So, I say it again, you have a destiny but that destiny is fulfilled by investing in the destinies of others. And this understanding should have a profound impact on how you choose a church, for you are not just choosing a place to sit and be worked on; you are choosing a portion of the body of Christ to serve with your gifts. This approach cuts across

> *You have a destiny, but your destiny is fulfilled by investing in the destinies of others.*

the silly hope of finding the perfect church. There is no such thing as perfection on earth and certainly not in a church. Instead, what you should be looking for is a covenanted body, a leadership team that has the goods for coaching you in Christ, and a place where you can invest yourself—from cleaning toilets to teaching what you know to organizing outreach to ministering in song. This is what it means to become part of that local portion of the body of Christ.

Once again, hold these truths up against your past church experience. If you have chosen a church unwisely, ask yourself if you made this mistake because you chose that particular body only for the good it would do you and not as a place where you could invest. Ask yourself if you entered into the relationship in a passive mode, like a patient sitting back in a dentist's chair. And ask yourself if your bad experience with the church wasn't due in part to your disappointment with their failure to fix you, with their inability to change your life while you sat idly by waiting for them to perform miracles in you. Yet, if this is so, perhaps things would have turned out better if you had joined the church to make a difference in the lives of others, knowing that this would open the door for healing and growth in your own life.

Hold this truth—*you have a destiny, but your destiny is fulfilled by investing in the destinies of others*—up against your past church experience. In fact, hold it up against your life. See if the call to invest in others doesn't change the way you think about how you live and how you connect with other believers.

Now, I have three practical bits of wisdom for you that I think you will need. From all my experience in helping people deal with church, I've learned that when these three truths are ignored, pain and wounding result. So forgive me as I say them as firmly as I can.

First—and please listen carefully to this—*a church is not primarily designed to provide you with friendships.* I know, I know: the church should be about love and unity and sweetness and light, so I ought to have friends if I attend one. Yes, friendships will naturally form when you and the church are fulfilling your functions, but the church's purpose is not to give you a social life.

This sounds harsh, I'm sure, but in telling you this now, I hope to save you pain later. Many folks I know expect the church to provide them with friends. So they go on Sunday morning to the church of their choice, they sit in the back, they involve themselves in nothing else, and six months later they leave the church reporting that it is a cold and unfriendly place.

Get this straight: You will have friends if you are friendly. You will have friends if you give yourself to others. You will have friends if you are pleasant to be around. And you will have friends if you are fun. No one else is responsible to make sure you have friends, least of all the church. What we need from churches is the equipping that empowers us to change the world. The church is not a dating agency or a party-planning service. You need to shift your expectations, let the church do its thing, and build your own friendships as you fulfill the calling of Christ.

One more thing about this. We can see from the life of Jesus that he had concentric circles of relationships. He didn't expect to be intensely intimate with everyone at the same level. He had his friendship with John; then he had a friendship with Peter, James, and John; then he had the twelve. Some say he had the twenty-four, he had the seventy, and then beyond that the multitudes. We have a habit of trying to be as intimate with the seventy or the multitudes as we are with the ones closest to us. It won't work. You should have a close circle of intimate friends. Then you should have a broader circle of people you see from time to time and enjoy but who aren't necessarily your closest buddies. And I say this here because if you are joining a church of two thousand and you expect for every member to be your best friend in a month, you are going to be sadly disappointed.

Go to church. Be friendly. Don't expect the church to create your social life. Be happy and generous and fun. Friends will arise as you pursue your purpose in Christ. Thus endeth the lesson.

The second practical truth is this: *you have to know your boundaries.* Joining a church is like attending a college rush night. There are a thousand organizations or clubs or ministries that all want what you do. They don't mean you any harm, they are just excited about their purpose and they want you to join in. And this is why church can be the biggest enemy of everything else you are called to be. There, I said it: if you don't know your boundaries, church can be the biggest enemy of everything else you are called to be.

Think about it. Take the average church of, say, five hundred. You sit there on Sunday morning and they let you know about fifteen different retreats and the needs in the nursery and how the men should gather on Saturday to dredge the pond and how there is a new class on marital bliss and how we need more ushers and counters and, by the way, if you have any skills with computers, we are doing something cool in the youth building and need your help. And you are a good guy and you want to pitch in. And so does your wife and your son. And, of course, your daughters seem to need to fly into the church every time the doors fly open.

Before long you don't have a family or a marriage or a personal life. You have an unpaid staff position at First Church.

Consider this: Paul said in 2 Corinthians 10:13 that he would not boast beyond what was appropriate in God, but would "confine our boasting to the field God has assigned to us, a field that reaches even to you." Clearly, Paul knew what God had assigned to him in that season of his life and he knew that this field of responsibility extended to the Corinthians. Presumably, he might have named other responsibilities and perhaps other churches or cities that were not within his field.

We can draw a principle from this. If we will ask, God will make clear to us what he has assigned to us for any season in our lives. And he will give grace for that field. To go beyond that field and grace is to do too much, to not have enough grace, and to experience burnout. To live in less than that field is to miss the growth and impact possible for our lives.

We have to know the field assigned to us and then have the courage to say no to what we aren't meant to do. Otherwise, we will always be responding to need and opportunity, and nowhere are need and opportunity more skillfully presented than in church. And this is as it should be, but you have to know who you are, what God has assigned you to do, and how you are meant to live. Yes, you should serve in the church where you attend, as I've said. But you have to prayerfully know where you are meant to invest yourself and where you are not. Then, you must have the courage to lovingly defend the God-ordained configuration of your life from that children's ministry coordinator who calls every night wanting your time. Got it?

Finally, this: *there may come a day, as there already probably has, when you will need to leave your church.* You will simply have to say good-bye. I hope it does not come, for I hope you are more whole now than you were and that you make a wiser choice. Still, it may become necessary to leave, and I want you to know how.

> **You have to know who you are, what God has assigned you to do, and how you are meant to live.**

We have a marvelous example of how to say good-bye in an Old Testament prophet. In 1 Samuel 12, we find Samuel saying farewell to Israel. The circumstances are not necessarily good. Israel has chosen a king and Samuel doesn't approve; he knows it is time for him to leave. Read this chapter. Samuel does not just leave without a word as many of us do, nor does he sign his resignation with flair and stir up trouble as he goes. Instead, he tries to make things clean. He asks if he has offended anyone or wronged them in any way. If he has, he is eager to make it right. He then reviews some history, not to complain but to remind his listeners how they arrived at this point. Then he commits to pray for the people and affirms that for him not to pray for them would be sin. And finally, he charges them to continue serving the Lord faithfully.

That's it. He takes his leave and goes. And I hold this up against the dramatic and damaging ways that I've seen Christians leave a church. I am sure God is often displeased by the way we do it. And I have wondered by the hour if the destructive way I've seen

Christians blast out of their churches of many years doesn't leave a residue in their lives that never lets them successfully settle in again. I believe the way you leave hangs over the way you live and the way you hope to belong to another church down the road. If you ever expect to find nobility and spiritual cleanliness when you reconnect in another church, conduct yourself nobly and cleanly when you leave your current church. There is an art to saying good-bye and I urge you to learn it in the hope that you will never need to practice that art again. I hope you have recovered who you are, that you have learned how to prayerfully choose a church again, and that now, full of confidence in God, you are ready to invest and lift a newfound people to their best.

The day of being mired in church hurt is over. Now it is time to belong to the team with which you will help to change your world.

Epilogue

AND SO WE COME TO THE END. But I began a story I have not finished, and we must grasp the meaning of it before we go.

You remember our tale of Mark, how he ran away at the arrest of Jesus and then later abandoned Paul and Barnabas on that first missionary journey? We left off with Barnabas and Mark sailing for Crete, with Paul starting his second missionary journey with a new team, and with the early church tainted by division and strife.

Thankfully, the story did not end there. You see, after all of his foolish mistakes, Mark spent some time on the isle of Crete growing up. His older cousin, Barnabas—that prophetic encourager, the one the apostles called "a good man, full of the Holy Spirit and faith"— was just the mentor Mark needed. So he stopped being that embarrassing weakling who ran away every time things got tough, and he became a man of character and spiritual strength.

To glimpse what happened next, we have to read between some lines in the New Testament. Picture it. It is nearly fifteen years after the Council of Jerusalem and the argument that caused Paul and Barnabas to go their separate ways. Now Paul is writing the conclusion of his letter to the Colossians. And we read these words: "My fellow prisoner Aristarchus sends you his greetings, as does Mark, the cousin of Barnabas."

What? Mark is back? But what happened?

We don't know, but clearly, Mark has returned from Crete, has been reconciled to Paul, and is now with him in Rome. And the reconciliation must have just happened when Paul wrote those words because he feels the need to whisper something to the Colossians. Having mentioned Mark to them, he says, "You have received instructions about him; if he comes to you, welcome him."[35] So, Paul wants the churches that were offended with Mark to welcome him again. How wonderful! The season of bitterness and anger has passed.

There is more. Sometime after his return, Mark must have served with Peter, because in 1 Peter 5:13, Peter refers to Mark as his "son." In fact, Peter's influence on Mark may have been quite profound. Scholars believe that Mark's Gospel gives evidence of Peter's influence, which means that the two men may have served the Lord together for years on end, all the while Mark absorbed Peter's memories of what it was like to walk at Jesus' side. It is pleasant to think about Mark, now back in good graces, learning of the Christ from this loving older man.

Finally, though, there is the mention of Mark that we find so tender as it brings the story near its end. It comes from 2 Timothy. We should remember that this is the last letter Paul ever writes. He will soon die and he senses it. We can tell from his tone and from the issues he chooses to address. And then, he says this, "Get Mark and bring him with you, because he is helpful to me in my ministry."[36] The aged apostle—having once been so furious with Mark, the one who let them all down—now has seen the change and needs Mark at his side.

"Get Mark," Paul writes shortly before his death. "He is helpful to me in my ministry." How much these words mean. How they reveal the change in both men and the triumph of forgiveness and grace. And how much the words must have meant to the still-healing soul of Mark.

Still, there is more. Mark continued to grow. Mentored by powerful men and made better by righteously confronting his mistakes, Mark emerged a lion of the faith. We know that he became the bishop of Alexandria. We know that he led his people well. We know, too, that there was persecution and that he was eventually killed for the faith. And we know that, as one church historian has said, the banner over Mark's life at the end was "This time, he did not run away."

Here, then, is the lesson: the bitterness and rage that threatened to split the church in those early days was, in time, healed—by mercy and grace and by men seeing the righteous potential in each other. And together they changed the world.

Now we must go and do likewise, for God did not give us the story of Mark in the Bible so we could scoff and shake our heads. He gave it to us so that we could see what is possible, so that we would know how to heal, and so that we could get on with the business of fulfilling our calling in this world.

You should know, too, that my story has begun to end on very much this same tone. While I was writing this book, I received a call from the chairman of those elders from whom I have long been estranged. We met, we apologized, we prayed together, and we shook hands in hopes of a better day.

As I drove home from that meeting, I did not feel a flood of relief or some tidal wave of loving emotion. No, most of that had come earlier as I battled to forgive. What I felt as I drove home was the unspeakable sense of waste, of the years lost and the friendships—which are rare in this world—at least suspended if not gone forever. And my tears were not for me, but for the Kingdom of God and the tragic squandering that it all has been. The hours, the potential, the partnerships for good—cast aside in our smallness and the need to win at our little games.

I close with the heartfelt sense that life is short, that the hour is desperate, and that our God is better than we allow him to be in our lives. We should go forth, then, clean and free, trophies of his grace, to offer the world what we have learned in our hours of pain. Perhaps, when all is said and done, this is the lasting meaning of what we've endured.

About the Author

Stephen Mansfield is the *New York Times* bestselling author of *The Faith of George W. Bush, Never Give In: The Extraordinary Character of Winston Churchill,* and *The Faith of Barack Obama,* among other works of history and biography. Founder of The Mansfield Group, a research and communications firm, and Chartwell Literary Group, which creates and manages literary projects, Stephen is also in wide demand as a lecturer and speaker. He lives in Nashville and Washington, DC, with his wife, Beverly, a successful producer and songwriter. For more information, visit MansfieldGroup.com.

Acknowledgments

A book this unusual required an unusual band of friends for guidance and I have had, thank God, just that. Jeff Pack was that perfect blend of coach and critic who made this book far better than it was. Dan Williamson wrestled with the ideal of forgiveness—and with me—in a manner that changed both my thinking and my heart. Chip Arnold gave me wise advice and input of the kind that only an elegant artist can give. Jonathan Rogers blessed me with the benefits of his years of literary success, and Flip Blaney not only approached the project as an eyewitness to my church hurt but also as a skilled psychologist. All of these have humbled me by their wisdom and honored me by standing at my side.

Esther Fedorkevich, agent and friend, has made my partnership with Tyndale House Publishers a joy. She also introduced me to George Barna, which has led not only to many episodes of good food and music, but also to a friendship that holds the promise of synergy through the years.

As enriched as I am by wise friends, I am even more so by being in love with a wise woman. Beverly, my wife, contended against my laziness, wordiness, and pride to make this book a better tool, and along the way helped make me a bit of a better man. I love her for these and all her gifts to me, but most of all because she simply exists.

While I was writing this book I was keenly aware that my friend of many years, Dr. George Grant, was going through the very type of torturous season that I describe in these pages. He will emerge better than before because he is a righteous man, but I will never be more inspired by his example than I am now. *Tu ne cede malis sed contra audentior ito*, my old friend.

Notes

1. Among the best of these are *Toxic Faith: Experiencing Healing from Painful Spiritual Abuse* by Stephen Arterburn and Jack Felton, and *Healing Spiritual Abuse: How to Break Free from Bad Church Experiences* by Ken Blue.
2. C. S. Lewis used this phrase in his marvelous Introduction to Athanasius's *On The Incarnation* (Crestwood, NY: St Vladimer's Seminary Press, 1993; originally published in 1944 by Centenary Press).
3. These and other moving Lincoln tales are found in Jim Bishop's *The Day Lincoln Was Shot* (New York: Gramercy Books, 1955, 1983).
4. Arnold A. Dallimore, *George Whitefield: The Life and Times of the Great Evangelist of the Eighteenth-Century Revival*, vol. 2 (Westchester, IL: Crossway Books, 1979), 23.
5. Arnold A. Dallimore, *George Whitefield: The Life and Times of the Great Evangelist of the Eighteenth-Century Revival*, vol. 1 (Westchester, IL: Cornerstone Books, 1970), 25.
6. Albert D. Belden, *George Whitefield, The Awakener* (Nashville, TN: Cokesbury Press, 1930), 55.
7. Frank Lambert, *Pedlar in Divinity: George Whitefield and the Transatlantic Revivals* (Princeton, NJ: Princeton University Press, 1994), 6.
8. Ibid., 46.
9. Ibid., 65.
10. John Pollock, *George Whitefield and the Great Awakening* (Herts, England: Lion Publishing, 1972), 173.
11. J. D. Walsh, "Wesley vs. Whitefield," *Christian History* 12, issue 38, no. 2 (April 1993): 34.
12. George Whitefield, *George Whitefield's Journals* (Edinburgh, Scotland: The Banner of Truth Trust, 1905), 17.

13. Frank Lambert, *Pedlar in Divinity*, 225.
14. Iain Murray, *Jonathan Edwards: A New Biography* (Carlisle: The Banner of Truth Trust, 1989), 340.
15. Ibid., 355.
16. Ibid., 380.
17. Ibid., 381.
18. Cathleen Falsani, "Bono's American Prayer," *Christianity Today* 47, no. 3 (March 2003), http://www.ctlibrary.com/ct/2003/march/2.38.html.
19. Ibid.
20. Jonah 2:8
21. 1 Samuel 19:2
22. 1 Samuel 19:4
23. 1 Samuel 20:4
24. 1 Samuel 20:33
25. 1 Samuel 23:16
26. 1 Samuel 23:17
27. Leviticus 16:21
28. Frederic Buechner, *Wishful Thinking* (New York: Harper & Row, 1973), 2.
29. 1 Thessalonians 3:3
30. Psalm 139:16
31. James 1:2-4, PHILLIPS
32. Psalm 119:71
33. Genesis 50:20
34. Luke 24:13-24, author's paraphrase
35. Colossians 4:10
36. 2 Timothy 4:11

Online Discussion *guide*

TAKE *your* TYNDALE READING EXPERIENCE *to the* NEXT LEVEL

A FREE discussion guide for this book is available at bookclubhub.net, perfect for sparking conversations in your book group or for digging deeper into the text on your own.

www.bookclubhub.net

You'll also find free discussion guides for other Tyndale books, e-newsletters, e-mail devotionals, virtual book tours, and more!

"Is this what Jesus told you guys to do?"

Light shows, fog machines, worship bands, offering plates—is this what Jesus intended? **Atheist Matt Casper wants to know.**

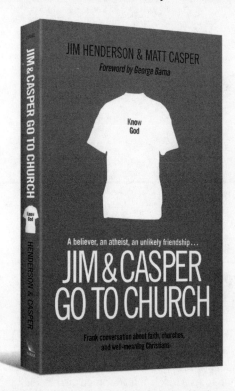

JIM HENDERSON & MATT CASPER

Foreword by George Barna

Know God

A believer, an atheist, an unlikely friendship...

JIM & CASPER GO TO CHURCH

Frank conversation about faith, churches, and well-meaning Christians

Longtime Christian Jim Henderson realized that he had no idea how a nonbeliever might interpret a usual Sunday service . . . or what might inspire him or her to come back.

So he decided to ask! Jim invited an atheist—Matt Casper—to visit twelve leading churches with him and give the "first impression" perspective of a nonbeliever. Follow along with Jim and Casper on their visits, and eavesdrop as they discuss what they found. Their articulate, sometimes humorous, and always insightful dialogue offers Christians a view of an environment where we've become overly comfortable: the church.

ISBN 978-1-4143-5858-1

WHY **MILLIONS** OF TODAY'S MOST COMMITTED
CHURCH MEMBERS MAY BE READY TO BOLT —
AND WHAT TO DO ABOUT IT.

the **resignation** of **eve**

WHAT IF ADAM'S RIB IS
NO LONGER WILLING TO BE
THE CHURCH'S BACKBONE?

jim henderson

In talking with women around the country, Jim Henderson has come
to believe there is an epidemic of quiet, even sad resignation among
dedicated Christian women who are feeling overworked and under-
valued in the church. As a result, many women are discouraged. Some,
particularly young women, respond by leaving the organized church . . .
or walking away from the faith altogether.

What does this mean for your church and for the body of Christ
as a whole?

Containing personal interviews with women and new research from
George Barna, *The Resignation of Eve* is a must-read, conversation-
starting book for women who have been engaged in the church, as
well as for their pastors and ministry leaders.

ISBN 978-1-4143-3730-2